To Hazel
Wishing
everythi   it   you
                              yourself

Leonard ...

Lyn. Matthews —
this book sent to
me!

Rollicking
Recollections

The rip-roaring teenage memoirs of
an English Boy in Kenya

Leonard J. Gill

National Library of Canada Cataloguing in Publication

Gill, Leonard J., 1930-
  Rollicking recollections / Len Gill.
ISBN 1-55395-655-9
  1. Gill, Leonard J., 1930- —Childhood and youth. 2. Kenya—Biography. I. Title.

DT433.576.G54A3 2003   967.62'03'092   C2003-902317-6

TRAFFORD

This book was published *on-demand* in cooperation with Trafford Publishing.
On-demand publishing is a unique process and service of making a book available for retail sale to the public taking advantage of on-demand manufacturing and Internet marketing.
On-demand publishing includes promotions, retail sales, manufacturing, order fulfilment, accounting and collecting royalties on behalf of the author.

Suite 6E, 2333 Government St., Victoria, B.C. V8T 4P4, CANADA
Phone   250-383-6864   Toll-free   1-888-232-4444 (Canada & US)
Fax   250-383-6804   E-mail   sales@trafford.com
Web site   www.trafford.com   TRAFFORD PUBLISHING IS A DIVISION OF TRAFFORD HOLDINGS LTD.
Trafford Catalogue #03-0018   www.trafford.com/robots/03-0018.html

10   9   8   7   6   5   4   3   2

Acknowledgments

My thanks and best regards go to the honorable lads I grew up with and fond memories of those who are no longer with us:

Alphabetically: Stan Bleazard, Don Elliott, George Henry*, Peter and Micky Jolley, Harry MacDonald*, the McCabe brothers - Brian, Dave* and Raymond*, John Poynder*, Rusty Russell, Tony Swain, Charles Szlapak, Pat Watson, Willie Young*, and all those who urged me, by their example, to follow the straight and narrow path, and guided me toward principles of decency.

Again, I thank artist, Jack Niswanger for his humorous cartoons which add so much to my narrative.

*Deceased at time of writing.

Dedication

This sequel to my first book, *Rambunctious Reflections,* is due to my dear wife, Kaye's, continuing encouragement. Without her help and inspiration, this book might not have been written. I suspect Kaye's enthusiasm is partly based on her desire to own a castle and to drive a Jaguar. I hope her dreams come true.

Rollicking Recollections

Table of Contents

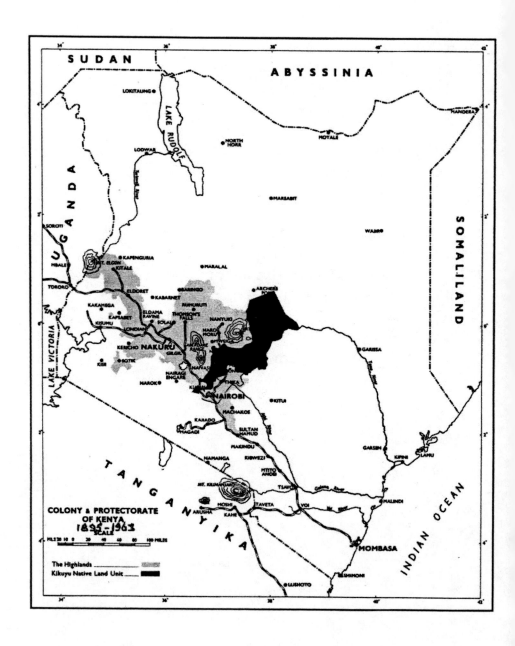

COLONY & PROTECTORATE
OF KENYA
1895-1963
SCALE

MLS 30 10 0   20   40   60   80   100 MILES

The Highlands ....
Kikuyu Native Land Unit ....

1

Holiday at Nyali

Clickety clack - clickety clack - clickety clack…went the wheels as our train rolled the last few miles to Mombasa. The three hundred mile trip would take fourteen hours, and we would drop almost 6,000 feet from Nairobi to sea level. Although we averaged just a little over 22 mph, there were times when the train rattled along at much higher speeds. We had stopped at several stations to take on water, mail and freight. I could sense the humidity and scents of the coast and knew we'd be in Mombasa in the next half hour.

"Who will see the first coconut palm?" I yelled as I rushed to the window. "I bet I see one before you, Elizabeth."

My twelve-year-old sister rolled her eyes up into her head, and looked at Mum as if to say, "What a child. Are we going to have to put up with him for the next month?" She was forever trying to act grown-up. I was too excited to bother with her.

"I can see a palm tree." I yelled. Elizabeth came to the window. "There," I pointed.

"Oh yeah, I can see it." Elizabeth was also excited. I refrained from claiming I'd seen the palm tree first. She had forgiven me for my earlier challenge, and I was not eager to provoke her again.

Dad was seldom able to get away from work when we went on our annual holiday at the coast. One year Mum took a beach cottage at a place called Nyali, some six miles from Mombasa. In those days, Nyali was undeveloped, but there were half a dozen rather basic beach cottages, each on its own five acre plot. Aunt Norah came with Mum, Elizabeth, Margaret and me. We went to Mombasa by train, taking Mum's little Ford car with us. We also took two servants.

We arrived on a Saturday morning at about 8 am and waited for the car to be off-loaded. Then we piled our luggage onto the hinged panel of the trunk, told the servants to await our return, and headed for Nyali.

The house was indeed basic, and had an outside privy some fifty feet from the house. The kitchen too was detached by about twenty feet. Having helped unload the car, I went to the privy to answer a short call of nature. The womenfolk went to explore the house, planning which bedroom was to be occupied by whom. On arrival at the privy, I discovered that it was full of maggots - millions of them. The seat consisted of a wooden box over a twenty foot deep pit. The insides of the box and the pit were seething with squirming maggots. I rushed first to the kitchen for a box of matches, and then to the car for a two gallon can of gas. Hastening back to the privy before any of the womenfolk needed to visit it, I poured two gallons of gas into the pit. Standing just outside the door, I flicked a lighted match into the pit and slammed the door.

Whooooosh! Off came the privy's corrugated iron roof, to land silently in long grass a few feet away. I peered inside. Gas was still burning in the pit with the occasional mild eruption of flame, but the maggots were no more. In a few moments the last of the flames died away, and the only evidence of the treatment I had given the privy was the lack of a roof.

WHOOOSH!

I put the gas can back in the car just as Mum came out to announce that she was going back into Mombasa to collect the servants and their baggage. I accompanied her. We returned to the house, and, with the servants, inspected the kitchen. We were not impressed. It was dark, ill equipped with no cupboards, dusty shelves, a rickety worktable, and a very old, stained sink with only a cold water faucet. Elizabeth and Norah informed Mum that the privy had no roof. I kept my mouth tight shut.

Mum now had to rush back into Mombasa to buy some groceries. When she got back with her purchases locked in the trunk, she found the trunk lock was jammed. We all had a go at trying to turn the key to no avail. So, back into Mombasa went Mum and I. We rushed to the Ford agents, and arrived as the whistle sounded for the end of the week's work. Mum had hurried into the workshop to report the problem we were having. The elderly Reception Officer was not happy. He had been looking forward to his first cold beer of the weekend.

He emerged from the workshop grumbling, "Where is the bloody car?" Mum pointed to the vehicle and handed him the key. He inserted the key and turned it without any difficulty. Mum was dumbfounded. "You must have tried to turn it the wrong way," snorted the Reception Officer, who clearly disbelieved Mum when she stammered that several of us had tried to turn the key both ways.

Mum decided to fill the gas tank, and I saw to this chore, refilling the two gallon can at the same time. Mum didn't see me carry out this job, so she never did learn why the privy had no roof. We motored back to the house at Nyali for a late lunch. The cook had managed to get the wood burning stove lit, and all seemed reasonably satisfactory. Naturally my sisters and I were keen to go for a swim, so after lunch we changed into our swimsuits and raced down to the beach.

We were faced with eight foot high stacks of rotting seaweed, piled at the high tide level all along the beach. The tide was low, exposing a thirty foot wide strip of reasonably seaweed-free sandy beach. The first thirty feet of water was a thick soup of more seaweed. Wading through this was not a pleasant experience, and my sisters were reluctant to enter the water. Eventually they followed me to clear water, shrieking their disgust as they waded through the seaweed soup.

We learned that there had been a terrible storm out to sea, and the seaweed had been torn from the sea bed and deposited along the beach. An Arab *dhow*, a coastal sailing vessel, carrying a treasure of silver East African 50 cent coins *(simuni)* had sunk in the storm. The coins were about the size of a U.S. 1 cent piece, and were the raw material for Arabian craftsmen to make silver bangles. The coins, washed up on the beach, were easy to spot as the salt in the sea combined with the silver to color the coins a vivid green. Over the next few days we collected several of these. Margaret was the champion collector, her bright young eyes picking out the silver chloride green better than the rest of us. Mind you, Margaret, aged about five, was closest to the sandy beach.

Also to be found on the beach were 100 pound bales of latex rubber. These had been the cargo of a British freighter which had been sunk by a German U-boat when plying between Ceylon (Sri Lanka) and South Africa. Anyone finding a bale could claim five pounds, and we searched assiduously, hoping to become millionaires, but we found only one.

After our first swim, my sisters and I returned to the house to report the condition of the beach. We were all a little depressed. Our holiday had not started well. That evening, sitting in the gloom of hurricane lamps, there being no electricity, we were startled by yells of *nyoka, nyoka,* (snake, snake) banging, and thumps from the back veranda. We rushed through the house to find that the servants had slaughtered a seven-foot-long snake, which had been seen as it writhed along under a table. What type it was, I have no idea, but we were all pleased that the servants had dispatched it with such alacrity.

But in the back of my mind was an old saying about where there is one snake, there is bound to be another. We had supper, and no sooner had the servants cleared away the supper table, than all hell was let loose again on the back veranda. Snake #1's mate had come looking for its spouse and had succumbed to the same treatment. Snake #2 was only slightly shorter than snake #1, and I was pleased that neither snake would slither into my bed during the night. I can see no beauty in any snake, irrespective of its length, color or demeanor. We retired that night wondering what else Nyali had in store for us.

Mum had a rather unusual brooch consisting of a two inch long platinum bar about one eighth of an inch square. In the middle of the bar was set a large diamond with two smaller diamonds on either side. It was elegant, valuable and Mum's favorite. She wore it all the time. One day, shortly after our arrival, Mum and Norah went for a walk along the beach. On their return to the house, Mum's brooch was missing. She was devastated.

Over the next two or three days, we searched for the brooch, but the tides swept the beach daily, bringing yet more seaweed, and the chances of finding it were remote. Mum had to accept the loss, and put it down to a holiday that was turning out to be more than a little miserable.

There was a glut of guavas - a soft, spherical, whitish, fleshy fruit with a heart of white seeds. Guavas are often used to make a delicious jelly. They are eaten raw or stewed, and can have the same effect on the bowels as figs. I like guavas, and ate far too many. I awoke one night with severe stomach cramps. I was about to rush to the privy when I heard the squawking of a petrified chicken. Since the nearest flock of chickens was at a neighboring house a quarter of a mile away, I wondered what was going on. I opened the back door and saw, in the bright moonlight, a leopard sitting guarding our privy door with a now dead chicken between his front paws. The sight of the leopard had a remarkable effect on my bowels. Instant constipation.

Mum came out of her bedroom to ask what I was doing. I explained, and together we peeked out the back door. The leopard regarded us malevolently. We closed the back door, and looked up at the top of the house walls. There was a two-foot gap all round between the top of the walls and the *makuti* (thatched roof), made from coconut palm leaves. We felt a lack of protection. We peered out again to see the leopard slinking off with the chicken in its jaws. We watched the animal until it was out of sight. My stomach cramps returned worse than ever. Nature's call had to be answered. I ran to the privy and exploded. I was back in the house within a couple of minutes. Mum had kept watch from the back veranda door. We returned to our beds. I was most relieved.

Aunt Norah is swept off her feet

Norah went for a walk along the beach. The raven haired beauty was never at the top of the class, having a lowish IQ, and being inclined to do some pretty daft things. On this occasion she forgot about tides. She set off along the beach, intent on a nice long walk. A gentle zephyr teased her long, wavy, black hair. The sun was warm on her shoulders. The wavelets lapping at the sand made a soothing sound. She strode forward, feeling strength in her legs. She swung her arms, lifted her head, and drew long breaths of contentment. She felt the sand between her toes, and the vigor of her stride increased. After about an hour, she thought about returning. Now she was walking with the breeze, and the sun felt a little too strong. She began to perspire, and was distressed to see the gap between the soupy sea and the cliff of seaweed narrowing quickly. She hurried, but soon had to walk through warm, sodden seaweed, swept

Aunt Nora was swept off her feet.

in with the tide. She hastened, her now tiring body demanding deep breaths of hot, humid air.

The tide continued to flow. Soon she had to run into the little inlets in the seaweed cliff, as seaweed-laden waves chased up the beach. In no time the water reached her knees, even in the inlets. But this was better than wading waist deep in the soup. The tide was still rising, and she was becoming desperate. She ran into one inlet and there was a man. And what a man. Very tall. Beautifully built. Blue eyes. Brown, short hair. Strong aquiline features and a warm, confident smile.

"Need a little help?" he asked in a friendly voice.

Norah's heart was skipping. He bent down and lifted her easily in strong arms, and waded through the rising tide, ignoring all but the lovely girl in his arms. Norah gazed up into his eyes, and he smiled gently down at her. When he reached the place below the house that I had cleared of seaweed a couple of days earlier, he set her down and with a low chuckle said, "You should be all right from here."

Norah swallowed hard, and invited him up to the house. He gallantly accepted her invitation. After climbing up through the soft sand to the front veranda, Norah turned, panting, not only from exertion, introduced herself, and thanked her savior fervently. Another warm, friendly chuckle and Captain Lawlers introduced himself. Mum came out onto the veranda, and saw Norah's flushed cheeks, glowing eyes and breathlessness. "Oh dear!" she thought to herself, knowing how easily her beautiful younger sister fell in and out of love. Norah stammered an introduction, and the seven-foot-two inch Adonis thrust out a huge hand that gently engulfed Mum's.

Suffice it to say that nothing could slow the burgeoning romance. Mum posed a lot of questions over the next few days, and Norah scuttled off each day to ask her Captain for the answers to Mum's questions. He was on leave from his British Army unit that was stationed in India. He would soon have to go back. Meanwhile, he was at a bit of a loose end. Norah saw to it that all loose ends were properly tied. She also found out the name of the town where his unit was stationed, and when he left, she followed, taking passage in a small freighter, which had accommodation for half a dozen passengers. Over the next months we learned from Norah's letters much of her story. After she returned from India, she told Mum more of her exploits. We children overheard more, perhaps, than we were supposed to. Armed with Norah's anecdotes, the following narrative emerges.

All the passengers shared the captain's table, and the little party was convivial, despite the danger of a possible U-boat attack. One evening Norah got into conversation with the middle-aged couple seated to her left.

"Are you going back to India?" asked the pompous husband, "Or are you going to India for the first time? We, that is my dear wife, Hermione, and I are old India hands." He turned to his wife. "Aren't we, my dear?"

"Oh, yes," agreed Hermione. "Dicky and I have been out in India for years," she added fruitily.

"I'm going there for the first time," answered Norah shyly.

"Oh, jolly good!" Dicky seemed unable to say anything below a shout.

"Where are you actually going?" he asked. Norah gave the name of the town she was aiming to get to just as quickly as she could.

"Oh, jolly good!" bellowed Dicky. "That's where we live."

"It's an army cantonment," explained Hermione. "Nothing else. Just an army cantonment."

"Yes. What are you going there for?" asked Dicky. "It's just an army cantonment," he added.

"I'm going to get married," said Norah coyly.

"Married," shouted Dicky. "Jolly good! Hear that Hermione? She's going to get married."

"Oh!" exclaimed Hermione excitedly. "To whom?"

"We know most of the chaps there," roared Dicky. "Who's the lucky blighter?"

"Yes. You must tell us," added Hermione.

"Captain Lawlers," said Norah.

"Oh!" said Dicky and Hermione together quietly. Dicky cleared his throat.

"What d'ya think of the trip so far?" asked Dicky of nobody in particular. "Bloody boat is too damned slow, if you ask me. Wretched sub will get us if we don't speed up a bit. Bloody U-boats!"

Norah was rather worried. Did Dicky and Hermione know something awful about Captain Lawlers? Over the following days she asked them, but they were evasive. Finally she got Hermione to one side on her own.

"You must tell me what's wrong with my intended." she insisted.

"You are such a lovely girl, and you really should know that Captain Lawlers has been married three times. All three wives have died in mysterious circumstances," said Hermione quietly.

Norah didn't marry Captain Lawlers.

*

But we must return to Nyali and our none-too-happy holiday. Mum was fed up. She had lost her favorite brooch. She was worried by her sister's impetuous behavior. The servants were upset about not being able to get their normal food. They were not altogether impressed with a fish diet, and the *posho* (maize meal) at the coast differed from that they enjoyed at home. The kitchen was not up to the standard they were used to. The roofless privy was unpopular. My sisters were not enjoying the sea, and we were all worried about further visits by snakes and leopards.

One night there was a very heavy rain storm. The roar of the rain on the *makuti* roof was surprisingly loud. There were several cracks, which we took to be lightning strikes, followed by crashes of thunder. The storm went on for hours but, as dawn approached, there was silence, except for the dripping of rain off the roof. At 6 am there was a knock at the back door. Mum got up and went to let in the servant with a welcome cup of early morning tea. No tea. The servant turned, and directed Mum's gaze to the kitchen. The kitchen was no more. Out of the rubble of the mud walls and *makuti* roof, rose a drunken metal chimney.

We could see by the hoof prints, a herd of huge Cape Buffalo had demolished our kitchen. Stampeded by the storm, they had crashed into the flimsy mud and wattle building and reduced it to rubble.

A look of determination spread over Mum's face. In no time we began packing, the servants with their baggage were transported to the railway station, there to await the departure of a train for Nairobi. On her return to Nyali, Mum found us still packing, and began to organize the loading of the car. Margaret decided that she would be out everybody's way if she took a last walk along the beach. She returned holding up Mum's brooch in her little hand. She had found it on the beach sticking up out of the sand. Her popularity rose to #1 on the Hit Parade.

The car packed, we piled in and left the scene of our unhappy holiday, thankful that we were all alive, and that Mum had her favorite brooch pinned to her blouse again. As we drove away, I looked back at the roofless privy and the metal chimney as it rose from the rubble of the buffalo-busted kitchen. There was a war on, and I imagined the scene to be not unlike bombed buildings.

2

The Makings of a Hunter

When I was nine years old, Dad bought a German-manufactured Hanel air rifle. Flocks of fruit-eating Coly or mousebirds were devouring the fruit in the garden. These drab brown, crested birds which are about thirteen inches long of which eight inches is a stiff, straight tail, are harmful pests. They peck all the fruit, eating little and leaving most of it damaged.

Dad spent considerable time tending the fruit trees and plants, and one year we had twenty-six varieties of fruit out of the garden, from avocados to raspberries. Clingstone peaches became a target for the mousebirds, and Dad tried numerous ways of countering their attacks including tying paper bags over bunches of fruit, smearing sticky banding grease on the branches, and laying mosquito netting over ground crops, all to no avail. Dad was an excellent marksman, and very quick to take aim and get off a shot. During WWI, a soldier in the British Light Artillery was expected to shoot with some accuracy while riding a horse or mule bareback at full gallop. Dad sighted his new Hanel air rifle so that it was accurate at fifty feet. During this operation he taught me how to take aim.

I suspect he thought that I wouldn't remember his instruction. A few weeks later, when we were strolling around the garden looking for mousebirds, he handed me the rifle and suggested I take a shot at a shirt hanging out to dry on the clothesline. From about thirty feet I put a pellet through a circular dark stain on the shirt. This pleased Dad - a little. The shirt belonged to the *mpishi* (cook) and Dad had to replace it - with a new one, without stains. "Lucky the *mpishi* wasn't in his shirt when you shot it," commented Dad with a grin.

During school vacations, I spent a lot of time shooting mousebirds, and became quite good at bushcraft: creeping up on the birds, and keeping my face averted until I was in position. Birds and animals become alarmed when they can see a hunter's face and eyes. I also learned that the mousebirds clustered together on tree branches as the sun sets, and are reluctant to fly away even when they are being picked off. As the light became too dim for shooting, I would have to give up. But I found that by filing off the bluing on the back of the foresight blade to provide a shiny tip, I could shoot accurately until later into the evening, maneuvering into a position from which the mousebirds were silhouetted against the evening sky.

My daily bag increased until the birds became less plentiful and more alert in our garden. This necessitated further bushcraft skill and shots from greater distances. I became adept at stalking and shooting with a high degree of accuracy. Joe, my little Fox-terrier, was a great help, distracting the pests as I stalked them, and charging in to retrieve dead birds which he dropped proudly at my feet.

Often Dad little had time for pest control, so I became the main bird shooter until Dad bought a light shotgun. The 'garden gun' fired a 9mm cartridge of very small pellets. It went off with quite a bang, but the shot didn't travel far and had little energy after about fifty feet. It was an ideal weapon to use against huddled mousebirds at sunset.

While I was attending boarding school, I was away from home nine months of the year - we had three terms of about three months each, with three vacations ranging from about three to six weeks. So it was the little 'garden gun' that Dad used when I was away at school. The air rifle was stored in a locked cupboard after cleaning and oiling, and remained my favorite weapon with which to shoot mousebirds.

Under Dad's instruction, the Hanel served as my introduction into hunting and shooting. He was an exceptionally patient teacher. The fact that he had not been successful in teaching Mum to play golf was due to her reluctance to waste time on such an inane activity. I, on the other hand, was a keen student and absorbed Dad's instruction avidly. I was not allowed to shoot at anything other than mousebirds, pigeons or a target card, which had to be set up in a safe place. The air rifle was not sufficiently powerful to drive a pellet through a bird, but I was taught to always be aware of what was on the far side of any target, in case I missed.

Dad never heard of the shooting incidents in which Bosom and I shot his parents' valuable gramophone records to pieces, and Bruce put a .22 'short' slug in my leg, but he taught me the rules of safe firearm handling. However, he never allowed me to have a .22 rifle, because he considered it too dangerous to use around residential areas. The Hanel air rifle and the 'Garden Gun' were safe to use around our three-acre garden (approximately 600 feet by 220 feet), if they were used responsibly. I found satisfaction in the sport, and knew that, if I behaved stupidly, I would not be allowed to continue to enjoy it. I went mousebird shooting most days when not at school. Neighbors, and the parents of friends, asked me to shoot mousebirds in their gardens, knowing that I was proficient and responsible.

As I grew up, I had some unforgettable hunting experiences. When I was twelve, an army captain friend of my parents asked me if I'd like to go on a day's crocodile hunting with him. I guess Dad had told him that I was becoming a competent shot and a good stalker. It was assumed that the captain would do the shooting. He took me by car to a river, where we walked quietly along the bank. I pointed out a croc lying on a sandbar in the river.

The captain, unable to make out the croc against the gray pebbles and sand, handed me the rifle, and told me to shoot the croc between the eyes. I took the double-barreled .470, crept closer, aimed and fired. I plugged the croc between the eyes, and after a massive spasm that made the huge reptile arc backwards, it collapsed in shallow water. I hadn't been told about the kick of the rifle, was knocked a couple of steps backwards, landing on my rump. The recoil of the .470 was far too heavy for a boy of twelve, and the captain should have had his rump kicked for putting it in my hands. I might well have suffered a broken cheek or collarbone. I was lucky to have got away with only severe bruising.

In moments, a number of tribesmen came to help skin the carcass, for which task they were paid by being given the meat. The tribesmen and the captain complimented me on my skill in stalking and marksmanship, which mitigated the embarrassing fall on my butt, and the pain in my shoulder that I was trying not to show.

Bedridden for Life?

On returning to Kenton after the holiday, I was walking naked from the locker room to the showers with all the nonchalance of a Masai warrior. Where I had a towel thrown over my shoulder, he would have had a red blanket over his. He would also have been carrying a spear and a shield. Supervising us that evening, was the Headmaster, Mr Cramb, who called me.

"Why are you limping, boy?" he asked.

"I'm not limping, sir," I replied indignantly.

"You are, boy," he said. "Come here." He led me to a long wooden table and instructed me to lie face down on it. He covered me with my towel and sent another boy to his office to get a measuring tape. He then marked a spot on my spine with his pen and, when the tape arrived, carefully measured from the ink spot to each heel.

"Hmm. Three quarters of an inch difference. Your left leg is three quarters of an inch longer than your right leg. Get showered and dressed and go to the sanitarium."

The school doctor came the next day, and diagnosed some rare condition. I was going to have to face being bedridden most of my life. In no circumstances was I to put a foot on the floor. If I had to go to the toilet, I must be carried. The condition was extremely serious.

My parents were informed, and Mum came to collect me. A couch was put out on the front veranda, and there I lay all day, being carried to my bed in the evening and back out on to the veranda each morning. Gitari, our house-servant, had to carry me to and from the loo and the bath room. It was very embarrassing for me. I hated it. The only good thing that happened over the weeks when I was laid up, was that I became interested in the birds that inhabited our garden. I borrowed Dad's field glasses, and Mum bought me a wonderful, well illustrated book on South African birds by Dr Austin Roberts. Most of the East African birds are in the book although the coloring of the plumage of some may vary slightly from those of the same species in South Africa. I have found enjoyment in bird watching ever since.

I was only twelve, and the thought of spending the rest of my life in bed did not amuse me. Nor did it amuse my parents and, after about six weeks, they determined to get a second opinion. Mum phoned the family doctor, William Boyle, who instructed her to bring me down to his surgery the following day. When Mum explained that the school doctor had said I was to keep off my feet, Doc Boyle told her not to worry. The drive would do me no harm.

17

My turn came and I was called in to see Doc Boyle. He immediately took me over to the window, and asked me to open my mouth wide. He gasped, took a pair of forceps, stuck them down my throat and caught hold of something.

"My goodness," he exclaimed, and called Mum to show her his discovery. My tonsils were in an extremely bad state, and would have to come out. The school doctor's diagnosis was completely wrong. My six weeks of having been laid up had been a waste of time, except that I had become interested in bird life.

Arrangements were soon made for me to go into the Maia Carberry Nursing Home, and a three hour operation relieved me of my rotten tonsils. Mum had been worried during the operation. Having trained as a nurse, she was aware that this minor operation would normally take a mere twenty minutes. Doc Boyle explained that the tonsils were so ulcerated that he'd had difficulty removing them completely. My whole body was toxic, and a gland in my left groin had been so infected that it led to the massive production of fluid which leaked into my hip joint and forced the ball out of the socket.

When I awoke after the operation, my throat and tongue were excruciatingly painful. The pain lasted for several days. I was allowed to leave the hospital to go home for ten days recuperation before returning to school. The toxemia was cured, and my hip joint went back into its housing. I no longer had an extra long leg. Mum held a party to celebrate my improvement, and vast quantities of Mum's artery clogging ice cream went a long way toward completing my recovery.

Wartime Tires

During WW II, tires manufactured in Britain were made using less latex rubber than in peacetime. Latex rubber had to be imported into U.K. from Ceylon (Sri Lanka), and ships risked U-boat attack. Kenya had to import tires, mostly from the U.K. The sub-standard tires were subject to blow-outs caused by over-heating, and casing failures from running over stones hidden in the dust on the earth roads.

Dad wore two hats, one as General Manager of the East African Timber Co-operative (Timsales) and the other as Assistant Timber Controller for East Africa. The latter appointment entitled him to a government car. He was issued with a 1942 Hudson which was not up to the tough conditions in East Africa. It had to have front suspension modifications, and had to be fitted with a larger radiator. A four bladed radiator fan replaced the smaller standard two-bladed one. The car had a propensity to monotonously blow-out right rear tires. We had fourteen blow-outs on one 310 mile journey from Nairobi to Mombasa.

We removed the back seats and put them in the trunk. While one of us drove, the other repaired tires in the back of the car. This entailed removal of the cover using tire irons, gluing a thick canvas-rubber gaiter over the blow-out hole inside the cover, repairing or replacing the tube, re-assembly and re-inflation using a foot-pump. I was more able at this job than Dad, who found being bent over for twenty minutes in a moving car a back-breaking task. During repair operations, we had to drive more slowly, but steady progress was made.

Back home, I spotted misalignment of the rear axle due to incorrect fitting of the rear right spring. This resulted in the rear right wheel running out of true, causing the tire to overheat and burst. Dad and I rectified this by jacking up the car, removing the spring, and re-installing it correctly. This solved a problem of burst tires that had plagued Dad for over two years. He regarded me as a reliable thirteen-year-old co-driver, expert tire repairer and an observant, practical mechanic.

Leaving Kenton

The time came for me to leave Kenton College and go on to secondary or high school. I felt I had done reasonably well at Kenton though my school reports continued to say 'Could do better' which I found a rather boring comment. I would have preferred they had said 'At least Leonard is consistent' and left it at that. But I had a grasp of English, arithmetic, geometry, algebra, Latin, French and geography. My knowledge of history was very poor as was my religious knowledge. I thought that the Acts of the Apostles was the weapon with which David slew Goliath. I was reasonably proficient at tennis, field hockey, soccer, cricket and rugby. I was better than average at boxing, sprinting and swimming. I was a good shot and not a bad hunter/stalker. I'd had chicken pox, German measles (rubella), measles, mumps, an appendectomy, a tonsillectomy and several broken bones.

3

Prince of Wales School

My high school was the 'Prince of Wales School (PoW also stood for Prisoner-of-War - which most of the students felt was an apt description). It was a government school with a not too good reputation, in part due to the inadequacies of many of the wartime teachers. Many of us would have been sent to Britain for secondary education, but the war made travel difficult and dangerous. The school was a mile up the road from our house, and I had to become a Stinker, (nick-name for a day-boy) as the school could not provide accommodation for all 800 pupils.

Discipline was, to some extent, in the hands of prefects. Sins of commission and omission led them to issue orders to write compositions of between 1,000 and 1,500 words. An alternative for more serious crimes was to be beaten.

***

I enjoyed school and writing, but not the essays some prefects demanded as a punishment for some minor offense. "Write 1,000 words on the velocity of a flea when sprayed by a Flit gun," they would say, or an equally ridiculous subject. I wrote 1,500 words on eggs after I had seen a 'short' at the cinema about egg production in 'batteries'. I had found the 'short' interesting, and wrote about it. I managed to retain the essay on every occasion after a prefect had read it. If they queried the subject, I always assured them that I had presented what they had asked for, and since I had to show them my work after a period of about a week, they could never remember what they had set. The pages became rather thumbed, but the prefects never really suspected my ruse which I employed for at least two years until I, myself, was appointed a prefect at the PoW school.

Dishy, Dirty and Dusty Teachers

Discipline was also enforced by teachers. They could send the offender to Headmaster which normally resulted in a beating. Lesser offenses attracted detention, which had to be supervised by a teacher, and was not popular among them as a consequence. One of our teachers was a Miss Bright. She was supposed to teach us English Language and English Literature. She was in her mid-twenties, very slim, pitifully endowed bosom-wise, and afflicted with a rather unsightly facial skin complaint. She had no idea how to keep control of a class of sixteen-year-old hooligans. We were studying Chaucer's Canterbury Tales, some passages of which are distinctly bawdy, and unsuitable for a young lady to teach a class of over-sexed, licentious louts. We were pitiless and insisted that she explain every wicked word and fruity phrase in detail. Her euphemistic synonyms and substitute phrases elicited hoots of ribald mirth, and Miss Bright blushed brightly. One day her patience snapped, and we were all put on detention the forthcoming Saturday.

Miss Bright didn't live at the school, and wasn't normally required to supervise Saturday afternoon detention. Thirty of us arrived outside the locked classrooms. Some of the Stinkers had come back to school on motorbikes after lunch at home, and entertained us with a show of grass track racing. Miss Bright arrived as a cloud of dust arose from the car park. Seeing us enjoying ourselves, raised Miss Bright's brightness, and she turned an unusual shade of puce. "Get into the classroom," she snapped and we, who already knew that the room was locked, suddenly became obsequiously courteous, and gestured her to lead the way. With a slightly smug smile, indicating that she thought she had us under control, she strode to the classroom door. On finding it locked, she spun round to find us all grinning. Apoplexy.

Miss Bright took a deep breath, and attempted to regain control of her emotions. Quietly, with teeth gritted, she asked, "Who has the key?" None of us knew, or rather, none of us was prepared to tell her. Miss Bright strode towards the teacher's common- room. We never discovered from whom she elicited the information that the key was in the possession of 'Moony' Barton, a stern teacher. Miss Bright strode back toward us, and instructed a boy to go to Mr Barton's house, a quarter of a mile away, and ask him for the key. Another boy asked if he could accompany his pal, and Miss Bright granted him permission. Together the two boys set off apace but as soon as they deemed that they were out of ear-shot, they slowed to a stroll. It took them 45 minutes to cover the round trip and, as the key was handed to Miss Bright, she was also given a message from 'Moony' Barton, who had had a gin induced afternoon siesta interrupted.

"In future, for God's sake, make sure you organize things properly if you are going to insist on keeping boys on detention on a Saturday afternoon, when Mr Barton wants to rest after a hard week, during which he has managed to keep his classes under tight control."

"He didn't say that!" Miss Bright was coloring again.

"Go and ask him, if you don't believe us," retorted the boy with apparent righteous indignation.

Miss Bright unlocked the classroom and we all shuffled in. She issued paper and pencils, and told us to write an essay on courtesy. Five minutes later, Clive

Hollyoak, one of the motor cyclists, got up, strolled up to Miss Bright, and threw his paper on her desk. He then headed for the door.

"Just where do you think you are going?" croaked Miss Bright.

"I've finished," grunted Clive.

"Get back to your desk," snapped Miss Bright. Clive shrugged and ambled back, sat down, and lolled in his chair in a show of utter boredom. Miss Bright then read out what Clive had written which amounted to about three sentences on Courtesy Cops, who thought they were God Almighty, and couldn't catch Clive on his souped up motor-bike. Meanwhile, I was writing a fairly sensible paragraph on courtesy to women. With an air of respect, I raised my hand, and Miss Bright asked me what I wanted.

"I think I've finished, Miss Bright," I said politely.

"Bring it up." She was slightly nonplussed by my polite demeanor. She read my composition.

"Quite good," she said. "You may go." With one accord the whole class sprang to their feet, charged up to Miss Bright, threw their papers onto her desk, and followed me out of the classroom. We had been in detention for no longer than twenty minutes. I was the hero of the day, and was slapped on the back and congratulated by my peers. I turned and looked back into the classroom to see Miss Bright glowing brightly - as appeared to be her wont.

Miss Bright and her sadly unattractive complexion, failed to appear the next term.

***

Another temporary teacher was a retired captain from an elite Hussar (light tank) Regiment. When we heard of his impending arrival, we expected to see a tall commanding figure who would stand for no nonsense. Instead, a rather wizened little man turned up, looking very nervous, cowering before us. He was so hopeless that I have difficulty in remembering what he was supposed to teach us. Our class of about twenty-four villains, with two exceptions, moved desks out of the way so that we could arrange our chairs in a circle at the back of the classroom The two less felonious pupils sat at the front of the class.

Out would come cigarettes, and we'd light up and chat. The seats of the chairs were filled with black horsehair, covered with hessian, and many of them were well worn, allowing the horse hair to burst out. One of the worst of us, Bob Archer, took a hank of horse hair from his chair, and stuffed it down the front of his shirt with a tuft sticking out like the hairs on a very hirsute chest. When our teacher gathered up sufficient courage to come down to our circle to inquire just what we thought we were doing, Bob rose to his full six foot height, shoved his hairy chest into the teacher's face and, in a deep voice, asked, "Do you want a fight?" The teacher fled back up onto his dais to continue to teach the two lads in the front of the class. We carried on smoking and chatting.

***

A totally inadequate teacher was *Chafu* (dirty) Johnson. Everything about him was dirty, from his clothing to his pasty white face. A small man, his clothes hung on him like a scarecrow. His oversized trousers were held up with a knotted tie and drooped to his shoes in folds. He reeked malodorously. He was a musician, and briefly our Choir Master. Standing on a stage, his feet precisely together, the toes of his shoes turned up, he conducted us by waving wildly with his arms. His choice of song was from Shakespeare:

Under the greenwood tree
Who loves to lie with me
And turn his merry note
Unto the sweet bird's throat.

To expect a mob of teen-aged louts to be enthusiastic over such a sonnet was asking too much. We were excited by the first couplet, thinking that Shakespeare was introducing a passionate, possibly pornographic, love scene. We were disappointed when the next lines turned it into an innocuous, insipid tableau. Boorish boredom.

Chafu had a four or five year-old son who helped the sanitary corps men to empty the buckets from the toilets of the lower members of the school staff - gardeners, grounds maintenance crews, cleaners and the like, who were housed on the school grounds, and had only primitive toilet facilities. The sanitary corps consisted of two men and an ox-drawn, two-wheeled cart carrying a steel tank into which the contents of the toilet buckets were slopped each day, for discharge into an underground cistern. It was a filthy job, and the fact that the Johnsons allowed their little boy to go round with the men, shocked us.

The family lived in a ground floor apartment beneath one of the dormitories. The apartment opened out onto a small formal garden which led onto a side-road that passed the main school building. *Chafu* always parked his car on the far side of this road, directly opposite his apartment. He parked it as far off the road as possible by putting two wheels in a shallow open storm drain.

His car was a small, ancient, poorly maintained, Austin sedan. It was well on the way to becoming a derelict, and luxuries like door catches had long given up the ghost to be replaced by cheap door bolts. Anticipating his car's early demise, *Chafu* never put more than a gallon of fuel in the tank, so that the petrol sloshed around the bottom.

The lads in the dormitory above *Chafu's* apartment would, after he and his family had locked themselves away for the night, lower a cord to friends who had sneaked out of the dormitory to wait below. They attached the cord to the car door, and undid the door bolt. They then hurried back up to the dormitory, where the other end of the cord was tied to the dormitory's balcony railing. Any boy, who awoke during the night, went out onto the balcony and pulled the cord, thus opening the car door. Letting go of the cord allowed the car door to slam shut. Bang! Pull, let go. Bang! Pull, let go. Bang! And so on, until a light in *Chafu's* apartment was switched on, and the apartment door opened. *Chafu's* shadow, falling across the garden could be seen from above as he peered into the darkness. Of course, as soon as the light downstairs was switched on, the boy above discontinued pulling the cord. After a few minutes *Chafu* would go back to bed, and the light would be switched off. After a few minutes, the banging of the car door would start again. On would come the light downstairs. *Chafu* never got to the bottom of this phenomenon.

Another little thing that was done to amuse *Chafu*, and distract him from his worldly worries, was the Coffee-Beans-in-the-Fuel-Tank Game. A handful of dry coffee beans in the always nearly-empty-tank, caused constant stoppages. *Chafu* played the organ every Sunday at a cathedral in town, some five miles from the school. To get to the cathedral was a down hill run almost all the way. Coming back was, of course, uphill all the way. Whenever *Chafu* put his foot hard down on the accelerator, petrol was drawn by the fuel pump from the tank to the carburetor. A coffee bean was sucked down to cover the exit from the gas tank to the pump, and would be kept there for as long as the motor demanded more fuel. The carburetor emptied, and fuel starvation caused the car to splutter to a stop. The coffee bean floated up, away from the exit from the gas tank. *Chafu* pressed the starter and, after a few moments, the carburetor filled again, the engine re-started, and the car would go another 400 yards before it again spluttered to a stop. The five mile journey from the cathedral back to school was done with about twenty stops. *Chafu* never got to the bottom of this problem either.

Chafu didn't last long at the PoW, and none of the other staff would take up residence in the apartment that he and his family vacated, as it stank so. Even after innumerable complete scrubbings, it took nine months to get rid of the stench.

PoWs go mountaineering and the PoW School gains a Latin Teacher

One Latin teacher had been a commandant of a prisoner-of-war camp in the foothills of Mount Kenya where Italian PoWs were incarcerated. A group of PoWs decided to climb Mount Kenya. Over a period, they collected tinned food, additional clothing, and blankets from which they made sleeping bags. They also made climbing boots and pitons, and acquired rope and all the necessities for a tough, rock climb, through ice and snow to an altitude of over 17,000 ft. They were all experienced mountain climbers, one or two being famous Alpinists. One night they escaped, and succeeded in climbing Mount Kenya from where they returned to give themselves up at the camp gate after several days of freedom. They hadn't been missed. One can imagine what may have happened when the sentry on guard escorted them to the prison commandant's office.

"We come to giva ourselves upa."

"Jolly good. Where have you come from? Abyssinia? Italian Somaliland? How did you get here? You haven't marched all the way surely?"

"We walka here."

"Good gracious! Jolly well done! Quite a trek, eh? What did you eat?"

"We tooka some tinned food. You know, from our rations."

"I see. How long did it take you? Several weeks I imagine."

"We taka nine days."

"Nine days . My goodness, that's unbelievable!"

"We good climbers."

"Climbers? What has that got to do with it? Oh, I see. You mean you have plenty of stamina."

"Stamina? Whassa that?"

At this point the escort enters the discussion.

"Sah. I think, Sah, that you will find, Sah, that these prisoners escaped from this camp and climbed Mount Kenya, Sah."

"Don't be silly man. That's impossible!"

"But Sah, I recognise the prisoners, Sah!"

The news got out that some prisoners-of-war had escaped from the camp unbeknown to Prison Commandant, Potts, until they returned to camp after nine days. This led to the prison director coming to the PoW School to teach Latin. He had no idea how to command our attention or keep control of the class.

***

One of my classmates, who sat directly in front of me, was an undisciplined lad, Doug, whose father had left his mother to raise Doug without the benefit of paternal authority. Doug was a strong, well built, healthy lad, who was all too frequently in trouble. He was good at sports, but academically he was a long way behind the rest of the class, and saw no reason to try to catch up. One day our ex-prisoner-of-war-camp-commandant-Latin-master, Mr Potts, (*Tumbo* - belly, because of his big beer paunch) came into the classroom wearing a very solemn expression.

"Today we are going to learn a very important Latin construction. You had better pay strict attention as, if you don't learn this, you will never progress in this subject." Then he went on, "I'm going to go through this once and then a second time, because it is so important. And should anyone want me to go through it a third time, I'll be happy to do so."

We listened attentively, and I have to admit that Tumbo took us through the construction very well and, by the time he had gone through it a second time, we were all sure that we understood it. Except for Doug, who was so far behind that he was lost from the outset. When Tumbo asked if anyone wanted him to go over the lesson a third time, I'm sure he would have done so quite happily - for anyone, except Doug. In all seriousness, Doug asked that Tumbo go over the lesson a third time, but our teacher was, with some justification, certain that Doug was, as usual, trying to pull a fast one. Tumbo strode down the classroom, caught hold of the short hairs on the side of Doug's head, and raised him to his feet, and then continued to pull upwards until Doug was on tiptoe. Suddenly Doug jerked his head away, and swung a clenched fist as hard as he could into Tumbo's big beer paunch.

The stricken master gasped and bent double with all the breath knocked out of him. Doug, as I have said, was a strong lad. Doubled over, Tumbo slowly lurched the length of classroom. When he had recovered his breath, he came back to Doug, grabbed his arm, dragged him to the door, and kicked him out across the veranda, down the steps onto a gravel path. Doug fell onto his hands and knees and, on getting up, found his hands and knees bleeding quite nicely. He strode straight to the headmaster's office. Holding his blood covered hands out palms upwards he said, "Look what Mr Potts did to me, sir." Tumbo lost his job.

*

Doug managed to unseat another incompetent teacher. This time it was Mr Anderson, who was supposed to teach us carpentry. We learned nothing other than how not to damage tools. Mr Anderson was overly fussy about the care of tools. It was painful for him to see a tool being abused - particularly by a ham-fisted lout. Wood planes were the most precious tools. One must never put a plane down on the bottom as the blade might get dulled. It had to be laid down on its side. Doug was idly planing the edge of a

31

piece of wood, chatting to the boy next to him. Unknown to him, there was a nail in the wood and as the plane passed backwards and forwards over it there was there was a clunk, clunk, clunk. The edge of the blade was having chunks knocked out of it.

Mr Anderson came up behind Doug, and couldn't believe his eyes or ears. He face became a muddy purple color. Froth formed around his lips. He grabbed the nearest weapon which was a 30 inch long piece of 2 inch wide plywood. He made to deal a blow to Doug's posterior, but Doug, seeing his neighbor's eyes open wide in horror, put his hands down on his unprotected sit-upon, which all too frequently was the target for chastisement. Down came the lath to strike Doug's exposed palms.

Unfortunately, there was a nail sticking through the plywood, and this penetrated Doug's right palm, and was torn out as Mr Anderson dragged the slat away. Doug didn't realise that his hand was bleeding. The teacher, still fuming, strode up the room toward his desk. Doug grabbed a narrow bladed chisel, and swung it from over his head in a chopping motion muttering something which started, "Silly old bast…" The blade flew out of the handle, shot past Mr Anderson's head, missing it by a hair's breadth, and stuck firmly in the chalkboard with a loud thump.

Doug's violent arm action had resulted in blood from his wound spreading far and wide, covering his hand. He left the workshop hurriedly, shaking his hand to encourage the spread of blood. He strode into the Headmaster's office, displayed his gory hand and said, "Look what Mr Anderson did to me, Sir." Mr Anderson lost his job.

***

In striking contrast to the temporary and usually worthless teachers, was the long time professional teacher, Moony Barton. A large, powerful, portly figure, Moony wore thick glasses making him resemble the Man in the

Moon. He had been a fine sportsman in his youth before he became myopic. He taught English Grammar, English Literature and Latin and stood no nonsense. He could be extremely sarcastic, and with a few words, take the wind out of the sails of any wise guy. It was advisable to pay attention, work at one's best, and do the prep he set. Otherwise he would show you up for what you were - a brainless, poorly educated, unmotivated oaf.

We were studying Shakespeare's Hamlet, and I and two pals were flicking screws of paper at one another across the classroom as Moony read passages aloud and explained them. His sixth sense told him someone was fooling about. He looked up, and caught all three of us in the act. He immediately had all three of us up on the dais dancing, crouched around the waste paper basket singing "Bubble, bubble, toil and trouble," in the falsetto voices of the three witches. This was not considered a macho thing to do, and we felt more than a little foolish, which was Moony's intention. Our behavior in Moony's classes improved.

***

An amusing and popular teacher was *Mzee Kobe* (pronounced M'zay Corbeh) Anderson. Mzee Kobe always wore a khaki colored, dusty solar helmet. He was a retired army officer, and had a deeply wrinkled neck from years of soldiering in the sun. This and his helmet led us to nickname him *Mzee Kobe* which is Kiswahili for old tortoise. He had a very severe stammer, but could read poetry and sing lustily without a hint of his affliction. He used to stride about the school, head sunk in a book, reading aloud long passages from Chaucer's Canterbury Tales.

His stammer was unlike any other, and it took him several minutes to get out what could normally be said in seconds. He told the following story about himself. Towards the end of his military service, he was detailed to train African soldiers in sentry duty. This included smartly presenting a rifle with bayonet fixed and shouting out, "Who goes there?" and "Pass friend." upon receiving the correct reply. Mzee Kobe had been into town to celebrate his approaching retirement from the army, and the apparent successful end to a training course for a squad of would-be sentries. Mzee Kobe and his comrades had imbibed a few beers, and as the driver drove them up to the camp gates, the sentry sprang out, bayonet at the ready and shouted out smartly, "Who goes there?" Mzee Kobe stood up in the topless Landrover and stammered: "Er um, H H H Hit er er um ler, er er um H H H Him er um ler a a a and er er G G G Goering." After a moment the sentry shouted "Pass friend." It is just possible the sentry recognized the stammer.

***

Samaki (Fish) Salmon was a Canadian who taught mathematics. It was extremely difficult to stay awake in his classes, as his Canadian drawl droned on and on, indicating his own boredom. He had gone through the same lectures so many times that they almost sent him to sleep. He would mark poor prep work with notations in the margin of the offending exercise book saying 'Keep out of the sun,' to avoid addled brains or 'Drink more lettuce juice,' to feed whatever brains we might have. In my own books he usually entered both pieces of advice.

At the end of the year, after we had all somehow passed our end of term exams in his subjects, he said, "Today we are not going to study math. Somehow I've managed to drum into your thick heads enough for you all to have done quite well in the tests, and to celebrate, I'm going to tell you about skiing in Canada." He spoke for 45 minutes, without an er, ah or um, about cross-country skiing holidays, and he had 100% of our attention for every minute. His own enthusiasm enthused us, and we all wished that we could all go to Canada with Samaki, so that he could take us cross-country skiing.

Occasionally a master would win. Early in a one-and-a-half hour session in the science laboratory, Dave and Robin were chatting. Teacher, 'Fud' Taylor was up on the dais explaining how an experiment was to be set up and conducted. Seeing Dave and Robin chatting, 'Fud', whose nickname was derived from the way he pronounced 'food', strode down the lab, and came up behind Dave without either Robin or Dave realizing the danger. 'Fud' punched Dave on the ear with a well aimed fist, which had the effect of concentrating Dave's mind. Robin's too. He leapt onto the workbench, and jumped down on the far side. 'Fud' ran round the end of the bench to get at Robin who merely vaulted back. 'Fud' made several vain attempts to reach Robin, finally gave up, and still fuming went back to his desk on the rostrum.

Everyone settled down, and were soon absorbed in carrying out the experiment. Dave nursed a thick ear. By the end of the ninety minute session, Robin had forgotten the incident. He collected his books, and was last to pass by 'Fud' who was cleaning the chalkboard. As Robin reached the wide open lab door, 'Fud' came down off the dais and planted his shoe with great vigor in Robin's backside. Robin was lifted off his feet and propelled at great speed through the door to crash into the passing Headmaster with a bone-shaking crunch. The Headmaster grabbed Robin, dragged him into his nearby office, and gave him four over the tail with his favorite cane. "That will teach you not to race about like a lunatic," said the Headmaster, puffing with exertion. 'Fud', who witnessed the Head's disciplinary measure was seen to smile, well satisfied that both felons had received due punishment. Not all our teachers were dopey.

***

Some of the boys at the Prince of Wales were rather older than their parents claimed. People, displaced from Europe due to the war, had had their education interrupted. Furthermore, their English needed to be improved, and by attending the PoW School, both their English and their education would benefit.

During a term when the main sport was track and field, the doctor visited the school one evening, and was taken by the headmaster down to the sportsfields. We were practicing various sports, and a group of us was trying to improve our ability at the Triple Jump pit. A Greek athlete was outstanding, and the doctor was heard to comment to the headmaster that the instructor was very good.

"He's not an instructor," said the headmaster. "He's one of the boys."

"Even taking early Mediterranean maturity into consideration, that boy is a man of not less than twenty-three," retorted the doctor.

"Yes, well he does come back after the school holidays with a very bushy mustache. We make him shave it off," murmured the headmaster leading the doctor away lest he embarrass the boy.

Another student was Van Rensburg, who was not a displaced person. He was just a little slow to learn, and was still attending the PoW at the age of twenty-one. One day, he and a pal, Brian, ran for the school bus as it pulled away from its parking space. It was five miles to Nairobi's center, and we were allowed to visit town to have our hair cut on Saturdays.

A school rule prohibited boarding or dismounting from the bus when it was moving. The headmaster saw the two pupils breaking this rule, and let out a yell, which could be heard for several miles. The bus driver pulled up, and the headmaster called the two culprits to his office. There he berated them for what seemed a long time, pointing out that they were seniors, and were supposed to give a good example to the younger lads. He gave Brian six over the tail with a cane. He then looked speculatively at Van Rensburg. "I can't cane you, Van Rensburg," he said, "you're a grown man."

Van Rensburg was overjoyed, but Brian felt a bit miffed at having been treated unfairly, until the headmaster grounded Van Rensburg for the rest of his time at the PoW School.

"But how am I going to get my hair cut, Sir?" asked Van Rensburg.

"Come to me," said the head rubbing his palms together in gleeful anticipation. "I'll cut your hair for you."

The next term, Van Rensburg came to school with his head shaven, and had no need to go to a barber - nor to the headmaster. Van Rensburg was allowed, by his parents, to leave school at the end of the year, when he turned twenty-two.

4

The Morgan Holiday

I was invited to spend a holiday with a school friend, John Morgan. John's father owned a farm and a saw-mill in the Kaptagat area, 150 miles west of Nairobi. The lumber business had led to a friendship between Mr. Morgan and Dad, and John went to Kenton College, where he and I became pals. The invitation to spend a holiday with John filled me with excited anticipation.

We explored the lumber-mill yard, and found a fifteen year old, derelict car parked in a clump of bushes. It obviously hadn't been used for years, and we decided to try to get it started. John said it belonged to his father, but couldn't remember when it had been abandoned. It would need a battery, petrol, and the tires needed to be inflated. No insurmountable problems according to John, who thought we might find a battery in the lumber-mill workshop and a tire pump in his Dad's car. So we decided to see if there was fuel in the tank. The gauge showed the tank to be empty, but perhaps the gauge was faulty. I took the petrol tank cap off, and peered into the tank. Darkness. I had a sniff. No smell. I took a box of matches from my pocket and lit one. Since I couldn't smell petrol, the chances were that the tank was completely empty. I held the burning match to the fuel tank filler mouth. Couldn't see any petrol. I lit another match, rocked the car and peered into the tank hoping that any fuel would slosh about, and the light from the match would reflect on its surface.

Whooooosh!

Yes, there were gas fumes in the tank. I lost my eyebrows and my eyelashes were singed. So was my forelock. Damn it! The old car was on fire. John and I slunk away through the bushes to watch the conflagration from a hundred yards away. It didn't take long for the old car and the bushes around it to burn away. Strangely, nobody seemed to notice the fire, until the tires began to burn, giving off black, odorous smoke. But by then there was little to save, and the bushes had more or less burnt out. The mill foreman went to have a look at the fire. He decided to let it take its course and returned to the mill.

John suggested I wash my face, and grunted without comment when I asked him if he thought anyone would notice the absence of eyebrows, singed eyelashes and forelock. We decided on a story of a camp fire flaring up suddenly, but this failed to convince Mr Morgan, who suggested we keep away from any other old cars that we might find. We agreed to this suggestion.

***

The logging area was up in the hills, and the logs were brought down on a light railway line. The rails could be taken up and re-laid to other areas, as logging requirements dictated. The wagons were pushed up to the logging area by a small steam locomotive, which then returned to the mill, where it was used to pull wagons around the mill yard. The loaded wagons up at the logging area ran back to the mill under gravity. John and I took the train up to the logging area, learning on the way all about steam engine driving, which seemed a simple job. At the logging area, we assisted the engine driver to load up with firewood, and waved a cheery good-bye when he left to go back to the mill while we went to help the loggers. We watched them climb up forest giants to lop the tops, and then descend to fell the trees. We learned 'all there was to know' about how to sharpen axes, how to make a deep cut on one side of a tree and a smaller cut on the other, in order to fell the tree, and where to cut a tree so that it fell in the chosen direction. In a couple of hours we had learned the loggers' jobs. In the minds of two 14-year-olds, it was all very simple really.

Then we went to see the fallen logs cut up into 12ft lengths by a mobile cross-cut circular saw, ready to be hauled to and loaded onto the rail wagons. All very simple really. We were told that the wagons, loaded with logs, ran down to the mill, gathering sufficient speed to run the last quarter mile over flat ground up to the forged steel buffers, provided the wagon brake was not applied with too much enthusiasm. Otherwise the wagons would stop before they reached the buffers, in which case the locomotive would have to be brought round to push the wagons the last few yards. This was to be avoided if possible.

Having learned all there was to know about axe sharpening, tree topping and felling, log handling and loading, we decided to take the now loaded wagons back to the mill. A worried looking foreman came to where we were seated on a pile of logs on a wagon.

"Perhaps you would like Karanja to come with you. He knows how to operate the brake pole. He'll help you."

"No, we won't need any help. We understand the task entirely." Braking was done by jamming a pole between a wagon frame and against a wheel.

"Yes, we'll be able to do that. No, no, we won't need any help." We yelled for the chocks to be taken from the wheels, and started the roll down to the mill.

We decided not to apply the brake, and the speed built up to a level that was quite exciting. We hurtled round corners, and logs crashed about alarmingly. Finally we were going too fast for the primitive brake to have much effect. When we did try to slow things a bit, the pole became so hot at its contact point on the wagon wheel that clouds of choking smoke hid the critical area, and we had to discontinue our efforts. We shot out of the forest at high speed, raced across the flat area, and crashed into the buffers, rather too heavily.

John and I sailed forward to land in a big clump of lantana, a wild member of the verbena family, which broke our fall nicely. We suffered only a few scratches. Well, a lot of scratches, actually. And our shirts were a bit torn. Well, very torn if you insist on the exact truth. And we carried the heavy scent of lantana. The logs had also left the wagons, fortunately taking a different flight path from that along which we had been propelled. The wagons were rather bent and the buffers were a twisted mass of steel, but the mill had its own workshop, and no doubt the blacksmiths would be able to straighten things out. So John and I crawled away through the lantana, circled the mill to walk out of the forest with the tale that the brake pole had broken, and we had jumped off the wagons fearing injury, even death. Mr. Morgan presented us with the unbroken but charred brake pole, and suggested we refrain from playing on the railway in future. We agreed to this suggestion too.

*＊＊

In order to keep us out of further trouble, Mr. Morgan invited us to accompany him and one of his African employees on a mission. The Survey Department of Kenya had sent him a map, and asked if he could find out the correct local name of a tract of land on the northwest section of the map. This was marked 'Poritupu' (empty grassland). At some time a government surveyor had presumably asked a tribesman the name of the place, and had been told, in Swahili, that the area was just empty grassland. He had entered the Swahili words 'pori tupu' on the map as one word, supposing it to be the local tribal name of the region.

Mr. Morgan drove along little-used tracks through forest, up into the hills to the north of the Kaptagat area. We came out of the forest onto rolling, grassy uplands. Mr. Morgan stopped the car, as he could now clearly see the area referred to on the map. In a valley below us there was a tribesman herding cattle. Mr. Morgan sent his employee down to ask the tribesman for the information he sought. After a few words, the tribesman and the employee climbed up to where we stood waiting.

"I understand you want to know the name of the area to the northwest," said the tribesman in perfect English in the rounded tones of an Oxford graduate. We staggered back. The tribesman was, indeed, an Oxford graduate. He had studied and practiced law for several years in England, having been chosen as young man of outstanding intelligence by his father's employer. All tuition and boarding costs, as well as pocket money, had been covered by his benefactor. After some years in a London law firm, he had returned to his homeland, to follow the uncomplicated life of a herdsman. He and Mr. Morgan had a long chat while John and I, with typical teenage disinterest, walked a couple of hundred paces along the track hoping to see some wildlife. Oribi, a dainty little antelope could occasionally be seen in the area. We saw one as it raced away from us, down into the valley where the herdsman's cattle were gathered grazing on the lush grass. When we returned to the car, the correct local name of the area had been noted on the map, and we left the herdsman with an invitation to call at the Morgan home any time he felt so inclined.

***

Friends of John Morgan on the next farm, two brothers, Roger and Robin, and a sister, Melissa, had a string of ponies, and we were invited to go over for a ride. I had never ridden a horse but, from watching others, it appeared easy enough. I struggled onto a mount amidst sniggers. I was advised to put my feet in the stirrups, and someone adjusted the leathers to the correct length. I had read a few Zane Grey and Louis Lamour books about the Wild West and horses, and I drove my heels into my mount with all the vigor of overconfidence born of ignorance. The wretched horse managed to get out from under me in a hurry, and I landed heavily on my back in the dust. Squeals of mirth, particularly from Melissa, increased my embarrassment, but I nonchalantly got to my feet, brushed myself off and started all over again. I suspected that the animal had been selected for its cussedness. I determined to master the mulish horse, and to insist I ride him on any future occasion. After a few hours I began to learn how to keep the horse under me and, after a few days, I was able to keep up with my pals as we rode over the farm, at full gallop on several occasions.

I was unseated hurriedly and inelegantly on another occasion when my horse took fright at the scent of a lion. Roger had drawn our attention to the lion, which was four hundred yards away. It was lying peacefully in the sun. We couldn't see the rest of the pride, but supposed them to be under a clump of bushes near where the lion lay. The wind shifted, all the horses took fright, and mine managed his trick of getting out from under me in a hurry, again. My friends caught and settled him. Stiff from my fall, I had to walk a quarter of a mile to where they were waiting for me, snickering at my discomfiture, particularly the sister, Melissa. I looked back over my shoulder to assure myself that the lion wasn't grinning, and licking his chops in anticipation of a meal - me. He didn't seem to be at all interested, for which I was truly thankful.

I remounted in scornful silence, and back in the saddle again, led the posse back to the farm house at full gallop. There I received a stern rebuke for galloping back to the stables. Horses must walk back home to allow them to cool off. Possibly there was more to horse riding than either Mr. Grey or Mr. Lamour wrote about in their books.

I must have missed something I'd found boring compared with the descriptions of the tawny haired, svelte girls that inhabited the Wild West.

***

Mr. Morgan took us on a hunt. I was given a U.S. Army Springfield .300 rifle to carry. John carried a light .22 rifle, and we set off on foot in the evening into the forest to a salt-lick. Animals would certainly gather there, and we should be able to bag a bushbuck by the light of the full moon. Mr. Morgan led us onto a mound overlooking the salt lick. There we spread out and lay down, determined to keep silent. I nestled the Springfield into my shoulder, and wondered how hard it would kick when fired. The evening was cool, but I felt warm in several pullovers that had been lent to me............. I dropped off to sleep, and missed all the excitement.

John had killed a bushbuck with a single shot. I hadn't wakened, even at the sound of the shot from the light rifle. I was finally awakened by a laughing father and his son. Mr. Morgan, a big strong man, heaved the bushbuck across his shoulders, and led the way back to the farmhouse. I followed in disconsolate silence, but Mrs. Morgan sympathized, and observed that I must have been very tired from so many new experiences. I was comforted, but was determined to show my skill at something before I returned home. My attempt to check the gas in the old car, the run down from the logging area, and my horse-riding efforts, had all blemished my reputation as a self-styled boy-of-many-talents, and to fall asleep on a hunting expedition - that was the last straw.

***

A chance to show my prowess came when I noticed a light motorcycle leaning against the sawmill office wall.

The machine hadn't been used for a long time, as evinced by the grass growing up around and through it. I made inquiries, and was told that it belonged to Mr. Patel, the mill bookkeeper. Mr. Patel was a quiet, very polite man, who regarded John and me askance. I asked him about his motorcycle, and he told me that the piston rings had broken when he omitted to add oil to the gas - it had a two-stroke engine. Mr. Patel had received new parts from Germany, but had never had them fitted as he would have had to get the machine to a motorcycle mechanic, and had been unable to do so. I offered to do the job, and Mr Patel, with some reluctance, handed me a carton of grease-paper wrapped parts. Shrugging his shoulders, he said I may as well have a go, as the machine would never run again anyway.

I quickly but carefully dismantled the little motor, cleaned it with kerosene, and fitted the new parts, taking great care to ensure correct tolerances and positioning of the new rings on the new piston. I assembled the motor, liberally lubricating all parts. After completing reassembly of the motor, I checked other working parts. The chain was dirty and required lubrication. The rear wheel was out of alignment, and the tires were soft. These, and several other things needed attention, and I rectified everything before filling the gas tank with the correct mixture.

The engine started after a couple of kicks, and an adjustment to the carburetor had the motor ticking over sweetly. Mr. Patel was standing at the top of the steps leading out of the office. I suggested he take the machine for a test ride. He came over, straddled the saddle and rode away. He returned ten minutes later, grinning broadly. Never had the machine performed so well. He had bought it secondhand from his brother, and had always been disappointed with the lack of power. It had misfired and spluttered more, in the opinion of Mr. Patel, than it should have. But with the new parts, a clean spark-plug and correctly adjusted spark-gap, it went up the hill from the lumber-yard like a bird.

Mr. Patel went home that evening on his motorcycle, instead of taking a lift with the mill foreman. He returned to work the next morning on his motorcycle, and announced that he had spent two hours the previous evening riding all over the area. His machine ran smoothly, and shot up hills with power to spare. It had started first kick in the morning, and he was delighted with it. He offered to pay for the work I'd done, but I refused, saying it had given me pleasure to carry out the job, and to know of his satisfaction.

Mr. Morgan was very surprised at my skill as a motorcycle mechanic, and John was also impressed. He told the horsy neighbors, and my reputation was, to some extent, repaired. Roger and Robin asked me to look at their father's car which wouldn't start. I did, under the gaze of Roger, Robin and Melissa, and within seconds I saw that a low tension wire to the distributor had come off. I found a nut in the farm workshop, reconnected the wire, and the car started immediately. The whole job took less than ten minutes, and I walked away smugly wiping my hands. I had been lucky to spot the fault so quickly. I now appeared to be a master mechanic, and the farmer came to thank me. He had had thoughts of having to get a mechanic out to repair his car. Most Kenya farmers are good all-round mechanics, but horsy folk seem to find all things mechanical a mystery and dangerous to life and limb.

The farmer took me horse-riding, and gave me several pointers. I became a confident rider, and the horse was unable to off-load me again. I doubt that my horse-riding skills impressed Melissa the sister, but I was now of the opinion that she was neither tawny haired nor particularly svelte.

Having thoroughly enjoyed my holiday, I returned home to face questions from Mum as to why I had no eyebrows, singed lashes and forelock, scratches all over my body, and a ruined shirt.

5

Fatality

Mum and Dad took us all on a fishing holiday on the western slopes of the Aberdare Range. The mountains rise to an altitude of nearly 13,000 feet, and run for some sixty miles north-south, forming part of the eastern rim of the Great Rift Valley. Streams running down from the mountain offer good trout fishing, and Dad was keen to try his skill. He considered that, at the age of fourteen, I was old enough for him to introduce me to a sport he loved.

We stayed at a bungalow owned by our family doctor. Dad and I went down to the river every day, and while Dad fished from one bank, I tried my luck from the other. We kept in sight of one another, and occasionally yelled when one of us caught a trout. One morning Elizabeth ran down to say a little Fox Terrier bitch had been bitten by a Puff-adder. The dog had been taken to the cottage by its owner, who was aware that the doctor kept anti-snake serum in a medicine cupboard. By the time we reached the cottage, the bitch was very distressed, and having great difficulty in breathing.

Dad had previously acquainted himself with the snake bite kit. In no time, he had injected the dog with a measured amount of anti-venom. She had attacked the Puff-adder from behind, not the thing to do with Puff-adders, which are slow to move forwards, but are extremely quick to strike backwards. The dog had been bitten over the left eye and the snake's fangs, on reaching the skull, had been pushed back to their full extent to deliver a full charge of venom. The little bitch stood no chance, and her tail soon ceased its brave, slow wag as she expired.

Dad was furious, especially when he heard the bitch had been nursing a litter of six, six-week-old pups. The owner, a young woman, told us she had seen the snake swim out to a large flat rock in the river. Dad muttered, "If only I had a gun."

"Oh, I have a twelve gauge shotgun," said the young lady. So, Dad and I followed her to her house, borrowed her gun and took the path down to where the snake had swum to the rock. It lay curled up on the slab, watching us with glittering eyes. Dad gave it both barrels of goose shot from twenty feet, which nearly blew it apart. I leapt into the shallow river, and when the snake had stopped writhing, picked it up by the tail to carry it over to Dad. He then told me that the area was known as Death Valley due to the number of fatalities from snake bites. He also told me not to mention this to Mum and my sisters, as it would only worry them.

We returned the gun and showed the owner our trophy. She grunted her satisfaction, and measured the badly damaged corpse. "Six feet, eight and a half inches. A King Puff-adder," she announced. "Not too many of them about, thank goodness." Dad and I returned to the cottage feeling satisfied that we had avenged the death of the bitch.

"Did you know this area is called Death Valley?" asked Mum mildly. "The lady who owned the poor little dog told me after I sent Elizabeth to call you up from the river."

"Well, I'm blessed," said Dad.

The following day saw Dad and me fishing again. I now watched carefully where I put my feet, and searched the branches over my head and in the undergrowth around me for anything that looked like a snake. Dad was probably concentrating on doing the same when he trod on a loose rock in the river. His feet shot up, and he fell backwards into the icy water, slamming his left arm against a sharp rock. He suffered a deep gash on the inside of his wrist. I had seen him fall, and splashed across the river to his aid. I helped him to his feet, and retrieved his fishing equipment while he washed his wound in the clear, cold water of the stream. He was in pain, having bruised his wrist as well as gashing it. We made our way slowly back to the cottage where Mum bandaged Dad's wrist while he had a warming cup of tea.

Crazy Australians

The next day Dad decided we had caught enough trout for a while, and announced we would all go over to meet his friend and business associate, Harold White, who lived with his wife and son a short distance away.

When we drove up to Harold White's farmhouse we found him outside, staring into the distance with his hand shielding his eyes from the bright sun.

"Where I come from, we call that a cow's trick," he muttered pointing to a huge cloud of smoke rising from the far side of a forest. "Hal," he said turning to Dad, "you can ride a horse. Come on, you too Len. We've got to try to catch those bastards."

Dad, who hadn't ridden a horse for over twenty five years, and suffering from a painful wrist, was about to demur. But Harold White turned and strode towards the stables, shouting for the grooms to saddle up, and for two other male guests to join in the chase. Dad found himself on a fast moving pony, racing through the forest, ducking under low branches, and swerving around trees as a member of a determined, hard-riding posse. Old, well-learned skills returned, and in his gratified surprise, he forgot his wound.

Worried that Dad might fall, I rode behind him but found that he was a better rider than I.

After three miles we raced out of the forest, and Harold White reined his horse to a halt in a cloud of dust. The rest of the posse also stopped, and the horses milled about in excitement. The cloud of smoke appeared as far away as it had been when we first saw it from the farmhouse. Harold White spat on the ground, whether in satisfaction or frustration, we were unable to tell. Harold wheeled his horse around, and led us back through the forest at a steady canter.

The other guests had been waiting anxiously at the farmhouse, and when they heard riders returning, they ran out to greet us. Harold explained that earlier that day he had evicted three men who had taken up residence in his workers' quarters, and had threatened his employees. If they reported their presence, the workers would jeopardize the lives of their families as well as their own. When he saw the smoke, Harold had incorrectly assumed the trespassers had taken their revenge in the form of arson. Later he discovered that they had left his property, and that the fire was eleven miles away. It had been started by honey hunters smoking bees from their hive.

Dad was jubilant at having found he could still ride, and that he had been able to keep up with the rest of the posse. But now his injury was throbbing painfully, though he tried to ignore the discomfort while he soaked up the acclamation from his family as I related his prowess and derring-do. I led him into the house, and poured him a beer. Mum made a sling and adjusted it so his arm was in the most comfortable position. Elizabeth and Margaret brought him plates of bread and cheese, and Dad regarded his family with twinkling eyes full love and of pride.

Harold White regularly held beer and cheese parties on Sundays when his house became full of garrulous, cheerful neighbors and strangers. Everyone was welcome, and Harold and his wife moved among the guests making sure that they wanted for nothing. It is doubtful if the hosts knew more than one in three of the beer swilling, cheese-and-onion guzzling invaders, but that was just the way the Aussies liked it.

Suddenly a farm worker burst into the crowded living room.

"Bwana, bwana. Memsahib alianguka indani dip ya ngombe." ("Sir, sir. A lady has fallen into the cattle dip".) Cattle dips are large, in-ground tanks. Cattle are driven from a pen, through a crush to plunge into the dip. They swim to the other end of the dip and walk up a ramp into another pen where they are held while they dry. In those days dips were filled with an arsenical solution to kill ticks. Cattle are immune to arsenic but human beings certainly are not. Struggling out of his jacket, Harold ran for the door, and raced headlong towards the dip. Without a pause, he dived into the filthy, toxic solution. His head shot up, and in a panic he hurriedly looked about him. "Wapi, wapi?" (Where, where), he inquired.

"Aaaaah, Bwana, memsahib akatoka kitambo!" (Oh, Sir, the lady got out some time ago.)

Harold hauled himself out of the dip, and went to shower. Arsenic can be absorbed though, and can burn the skin. Enquiries elicited the information that the lady had slithered down the dip's ramp and had only gotten her legs wet. She had also showered, borrowed some clothes from Mrs. White, and had been taken home to sleep off the effects of a little too much beer. As for Harold, he emerged from his bedroom, freshly showered, in clean clothes, his hair slicked down and wearing a broad grin. The guests toasted his heroism with another gulp of beer, and a mouthful of cheese and onion on bread.

A trip to remember

Harold White was chosen by members of the East African Timber Co-operative Society (Timsales) to represent them at an important world conference to be held in Washington, DC in 1947. He was to fly from Nairobi to Khartoum in the Sudan, take a boat down the Nile to Cairo where he was to stay a few days before proceeding down the Nile to Alexandria. From there he was to take a ship to Marseilles, and then a train across France to Cherbourg to embark on the Queen Mary to cross the Atlantic to New York. His itinerary included a rail trip to San Francisco, a Greyhound coach to Southern California, and then by hired car, back across the continent to Washington for the conference.

Harold was expected to keep a detailed, written account of his voyage by his envious co-members of Timsales. He was to take plenty of photographs, and be prepared to describe his adventures at a party to be held at our house upon his return. These requirements Harold met with an enthusiasm and humor that should have been tape recorded. When he came to tell his tale at our home, I sat cross-legged on the lounge carpet, my chin cupped in my palm, rapt in Harold's narrative.

When he arrived at Cairo, Harold decided to engage the services of a street ragamuffin as a guide. Ali and Harold became friends when Ali discovered that Harold was not an Englishman but an Aussie. Ali had no time for the pomes, as Aussies call Brits, but he respected the Australians. During WWII there had been a large military motor vehicle parts depot near Cairo, and Ali and his friends frequently raided the store under cover of darkness to purloin parts for Cairo's aging automobiles.

When the Brits were in charge of the warehouse, Ali and his friends, when caught, faced months of bureaucratic enquiries, to be followed by three months in jail if found guilty. Since his nefarious occupation frequently led to Ali's arrest, he found considerable time was wasted in attending court and when he was incarcerated. When the store was taken over by the Aussies, summary justice in the form of a hearty kick in the pants became the order of the day. To Ali and his gang, a friendly, if hearty, kick was preferable to boring British bureaucracy. Harold had wondered how he, an Australian, would get on in foreign parts, and Ali's friendship gave him great confidence, which colored his attitudes and behaviour for the rest of the trip. He would be able to act naturally, deferring to no man.

On arrival at Marseilles on a Saturday a little before noon, he disembarked, and slowly made his way to the immigration officers who were lined up behind a counter checking passports. Harold was in no hurry - his train for Cherbourg wasn't leaving until that evening - so he was among the last of the passengers to breast up to the immigration officers' counter. He handed over his Australian passport. After glancing at it, the junior immigration officer (JIO) proffered it to Harold.

"Sorry, M'sieu, you cannot enter France".

"Why's that?" asked Harold, ignoring the proffered passport.

"M'sieu, you cannot enter France, you have no visa," explained the JIO, impatiently shaking the passport in Harold's face.

"How long will that take to fix?" Harold had no use for a visa-less passport, so he continued to ignore it.

The JIO shrugged in true Gallic style. "Mais M'sieu, c'est impossible. You cannot enter France without a visa. You must go back to your ship. You have no visa." He slammed the unwanted passport on the counter with finality. Harold ignored it.

"How long will that take to fix?" he asked quietly.

Twenty minutes later, the problem remained unresolved. Harold still wanted to know how long it would take to fix a visa, and the Frenchman had lost all his cool. Harold switched tactics.

"What's today?"

"Today is Saturday, M'sieu."

"What time do you get off?"

54

"I will be relieved at 12.30." The officer glanced at his watch. It was 12.17.

"Go home to lunch, do you?" asked Harold.

"Oui, M'sieu. I go home to my family and we have luncheon."

"So, you're married then?"

"Oui, M'sieu. I have a wife and two children." Though time was slipping by, the JIO was happy to tell Harold about his family, and was about to elaborate when Harold interrupted.

"You'd better phone her."

"Phone who, M'sieu?"

"Your wife."

"Why should I phone my wife, M'sieu?"

"To tell her you're going to be late for lunch today. Tell you what. Why don't you call your superior to handle my case? Then you can go home."

The JIO gestured with his index finger and nodded in agreement. He strode away and returned immediately with a senior immigration officer (SIO). He picked up the passport, and showed it to the SIO who glanced at it.

"M'sieu, I cannot allow you to enter France. You have no visa."

"How long will that take to fix?" asked Harold patiently.

The JIO slipped away to take luncheon with his family. Harold and his new adversary proceeded along the interminable familiar-to-Harold conversation. Harold added the fact that he didn't want to enter France, he merely wanted to take the train across France to Cherbourg to catch the Queen Mary to go to America to attend a very important world conference. The SIO was not impressed. Harold reverted to his previously successful tactic.

"What's today?"

"Today is Saturday, M'sieu," replied the SIO, relieved at the change from the problem of a visa.

"What time do you get off?"

"I will   be relieved at 12.30." He glanced at his watch. It was already 12.39.

"Perhaps you should phone your wife to tell her that you will be late for lunch today........................."

Harold suggested that the Chief Immigration Officer for the Port of Marseilles be enlisted to deal with his case, and this seemed to the SIO a very good idea. The CIO was called, and the whole conversation started anew. The now tired SIO slipped away to a late luncheon.

After a full half hour of frustration with an Australian who just didn't seem to understand the bureaucratic necessity for a visa, the CIO took a deep breath, glanced right and left like a criminal about to commit an illegal act, and asked Harold to accompany him. Quickly he led the way through Customs to collect Harold's baggage, and then down corridors of immigration offices out to a car park. He ushered Harold into a big, shiny, senior government official's car, and drove him straight to the rail station.

He took Harold past all the ticket formalities, onto the platform, and saw him into a first class compartment. After a quick word with the train's conductor, and after giving firm instructions to Harold that, in no circumstances, was he to set foot in France until the conductor took him off the train to embark on the Queen Mary, the CIO departed. He left a satisfied and amused Aussie sitting relaxed in a comfortable seat in a first class compartment, ready to depart on a free rail trip across France to Cherbourg.

**

Harold had little to say about his trans-Atlantic voyage on the Queen Mary, and the rail trip from New York to San Francisco was only remarkable in that the train seemed to leap from one side of the rails to the other, with the wheels running on the ties instead of the rails. The Golden Gate Bridge was not up to Australian bridges, as it couldn't be crossed by trains. The Sidney Bridge is better in this respect.

However, Harold was impressed by the car trip from Southern California back east to Washington, D.C. This was done in a comfortable, powerful American car in the company of three other lumbermen who were also to attend the conference. They took turns at the wheel, and drove huge distances each day. Such distances were not possible on Kenya's rough, dusty, earth roads. In America, the roads were wide, smooth and well maintained. Harold opined that the car's ten gallon tank could have been changed, with advantage, to a very much larger one, as they had to pull into gas stations rather too frequently. But they managed to cover nearly 1,000 miles each day.

***

On reaching Washington they all stayed at one hotel full of others attending the conference. Harold and his friends breakfasted early, and emerged from the hotel into a waiting cab to be taken to the conference hall. On their arrival, another cab was standing directly in front of the impressive portals. Their cab driver asked them to wait, got out of the car, and walked to the other cab. His gestures indicated that he was peremptorily ordering his colleague to remove his vehicle. It was apparent that he was told, just as peremptorily, to do impossible things to himself. The altercation developed into a fracas, then a fist fight. Finally Harold's party was driven a further twenty feet so that they were directly in front of the great doors. Their cabby had, in his own opinion, earned a handsome tip.

***

What was it that impressed Harold most about America? New York? Cross-continental trains? Route 66? Large, comfortable cars? Determined cabbies? Yes, yes, yes.

But there was one thing that was particularly outstanding. American sky pointers, as Harold named them. The fashion at the time demanded firm, well formed bosoms, and the bras of the day were designed to make mountains out of molehills, and ensure that nipples jutted skywards..... well, perked purposefully. They were not shy, but peaked prettily, much to Harold's titillation. He returned home with a bunch of bras for his outstanding wife.

Another crazy Australian

Another of my father's sawmiller friends was Bill Murton, who invited me to stay during the school holidays. Bill was from Western Australia and, like many Australians was hard working, mad about cricket, and well able to look after himself whatever the problem. After work at the end of the week, Bill liked to sink a few cold beers. Late one evening he, his wife, Kathleen, and I, were sitting on the veranda overlooking a beautifully manicured lawn, edged with flower beds. The scent of the many flowers Kathleen managed to grow in profusion was almost overpowering. Bill had had a few beers and was fully relaxed as we chatted quietly over the events of the week. During a lull in the conversation, Bill's gaze wandered over the flower beds where he could see the colors of the blooms in the bright moonlight.

Suddenly we saw a leopard lurking in the shrubbery to our left. The leopard seemed to be blinded by the lights from the house falling across the garden. Crouching low, the leopard slowly made its way to the center of the lawn. Kathleen had also seen the magnificent animal, and was holding her breath in wonder. Keeping his head turned away from us, the leopard paused for a moment, and then continued to creep towards the right side of the lawn. Very slowly Bill pushed himself up out of his chair, and headed for the steps leading down from the veranda onto the grass.

"What the heck do you think you're going to do?" asked Kathleen. The startled leopard darted away.

"Damn it, Kathleen. You've frightened the thing. Now I'll never know!"

"Know what?" asked Kathleen.

"If a cat pulls in the opposite direction if you grab its tail," explained Bill.

"You were going out there to grab that leopard's tail?" Kathleen couldn't believe her ears. I assumed that Bill was just behaving like any Australian - prone to do crazy things.

"Yes. What else?" queried Bill, surprised that we should find bizarre, his eager aspiration to test a theory.

"Couldn't you test your idea on one of our cats?" asked Kathleen. "A little less dangerous, I'd have thought," she observed. I silently agreed.

"Well, it seemed like a good idea at the time." Bill was not convinced that pet cats were worthy of consideration for such an experiment. He considered he'd missed the chance of a lifetime.

"You've had enough beer. That, or you're getting daft in your old age," commented Kathleen. Bill went into the lounge for another bottle of beer, just to show her that his judgment was not impaired by the beer. He saw Mitzi the cat lying stretched out on the lounge carpet. He bent down and pulled Mitzi's tail. The cat awoke with a caterwaul, and lashed out at Bill's hand scratching it deeply. Bill cursed under his breath, grabbed a bottle of beer, and returned to the veranda.

"What was that squawk?" asked Kathleen.

"Damned cat scratched me," snapped Bill.

"Well, you shouldn't go around pulling cat's tails," advised Kathleen smugly.

"Yeah, well........." said Bill taking a swig. We chuckled, and the subject was dropped.

6

Shooting on game control

From the age of fifteen, most of my game shooting was on private farmland, much of it to eliminate marauding animals, man-killers and livestock attackers, or to drive off intruding wildlife, usually by killing one beast and leaving, the carcass on their trail to deter further visits by the herd.

On one occasion, during a serious drought, a herd of zebra continuously broke through fences to get to a dam, which the rancher had built to conserve water for his cattle during drought conditions. The zebra had been chased off several times, and on the last occasion a group of us on horseback had chased them at a canter for twenty-five miles, firing Boer War German-made Mauser rifles into the air. The old rifles and ammunition were kept by the farmer for just such occasions. We rested the horses by a stream before riding slowly back to the farm. The horses were given a rub down before we sat down to a cup of tea. Two days later the zebra were back, after breaking through a barbed wire fence. Besides drinking water reserved for the cattle, Zebras are always parasite infested and spread tick-borne diseases.

A decision was made to deal with the herd. Five of us, including an adult farm employee in the form of an Italian prisoner-of-war, rose at 4:00am, dressed, and made our way quietly down to the dam. We spread ourselves along the dam wall, and charged our rifle magazines, slid a round into the breach, and lay in wait.

As the sun rose at about 5:30am, the zebra herd came down to drink. We lay poised, safety catches off, waiting for the signal from the Italian, who was to shoot first. I was second on the left and aimed at the zebra second from the left as they spread out along the water's edge on the far side of the dam. The light quickly improved, and as soon as it was bright enough for shooting, the Italian fired. A fusillade immediately followed, and we continued shooting as quickly as possible. I was aiming for neck shots as a high neck shot is certain to cause immediate death. Moments later, the shooting stopped and twenty-one zebra lay dead. After inspection most of the meat was given to the farm workers, and the rest was sent to feed police dogs. The hides were tanned and sold to cover the cost of the ammunition. The Italian PoW was rewarded with a case of wine.

Many Italians, compelled to serve in their army, were reluctant to support Mussolini's expansionist aims and disagreed with his allegiance to the Nazi, Hitler. They surrendered in droves to the British army during the Abyssinian Campaign, and later during the North African Campaign. Most were skilled artisans and craftsmen, and some had farming experience. As prisoners-of-war in Kenya, they worked in industries and on farms, and many elected to stay in Kenya after the war, bringing their families out to join them, often at the generosity of the settlers for whom they had worked when in captivity. They were hard-working, and many did well, making a real contribution to the development of the British colony where they were well-liked and respected.

A trip to the Salt Pans

Dad often took me on business trips during school vacations. I looked forward to these journeys as a comradeship grew between us. We usually visited lumber mills where I could race up and down huge heaps of sawdust, watch the progress of logs being milled into lumber, and enjoy the scent of freshly cut wood while Dad discussed business with the mill owner. This journey was to be a new experience. We started out early on a long trip to visit salt pans on the coast some seventy-five miles north of Mombasa. We were to take a short-cut through African farmland to bypass Mombasa by motoring along narrow, little used earth roads to Malindi. That year the road from Nairobi to Mombasa was in an appalling state due to a drought. Many parts of the road were six to eight inches deep in fine dust. We had to cover a total of 355 miles to reach our destination, and Dad wanted to ensure the tires didn't overheat, so we drove slowly, and halted every fifty miles to allow the tires to cool.

These measures resulted in our reaching the short-cut turn-off from the main Nairobi-Mombasa road after sunset. As we progressed along the narrow road, we came upon forks in the road not shown on the road map. During WWII all the road signs had been taken down so as to confuse the enemy should there be an invasion. The measure certainly confused us. We decided to take whichever fork looked the most used, but were unsure that we were on the correct route. We had to stop frequently so that I could walk with a flashlight a few hundred yards to determine which fork I thought the most used. Progress was slow, and we both began to suffer eye-strain and tiredness. We had been on the road for over twelve hours.

Dad was gifted with the ability to take cat-naps. He could drop off immediately, to awaken, refreshed, after whatever period he had predetermined. He now thought it prudent that we stop to take a half-hour snooze. The night was warm, and the car windows were rolled down. It was a relief to shut our eyes, and lean back in dead silence after the roar of the engine and the rumbling of the tires on the rough road. Within a minute I could hear Dad's regular heavy breathing, and knew he was fast asleep. But, within another minute came the whine of mosquitoes. They came in dozens, then hundreds. It was almost impossible to keep them from turning the moment into a banquet. I was reluctant to be entrée to their feast, so I woke Dad who immediately grasped the situation, and we set off again with the headlights cutting a swathe through the near darkness. The mosquitoes were wafted out of the car by the rush of air through the open windows.

We rounded a bend and saw, some distance ahead, the tops of trees lit up by a fire. Dad stopped, not wishing to drive through a bush fire. We couldn't see the base of the fire which was hidden by trees and bends in the road, but we could hear the beating of drums, the cacophony of horns, bells, cymbals, marimbas and singing. People were enjoying an *ngoma* (dance) and this would be accompanied by plenty of *tembo* (palm wine) and *pombe* (beer made from various grains, usually corn, or fruit). These occasions were strictly limited by the Colonial Administration. Why this was so is moot. Things did sometimes get a bit out of hand, and revelers suffered injury or worse, but as is so often the case, had they been allowed to hold *ngomas* more frequently, the revelers would probably have behaved better.

After a moment or two of silence, Dad dowsed the lights, and we crept slowly forward through the darkness. The road snaked to the right and then to the left. As we rounded a bend we were a mere 100 feet from the *ngoma*. For a few seconds the dancers danced, and the musicians played on. Then someone spotted our car. A shout went up, and there was a wild rush for the bushes. We suspected the *ngoma* was an illegal one. Silence ensued, but for the crackling fire. Dad drove slowly forward and the full moon, hidden all that night, suddenly smiled down brightly as the clouds sailed away on a warm breeze. We halted, and after a few moments a near naked man appeared out of the bushes, and walked up to the car grinning a little guiltily, confirming our suspicions that permission had not been granted for the *ngoma*. He was a magnificent specimen, and his broad chest heaved from the exertion of the dance. His body, covered in perspiration, gleamed in the moonlight, and was silhouetted against the blazing fire. Dad smiled, and asked if we were on the right road for Malindi. *Naam, ni safari ya siku moja.* (Yes, it is a journey of one day). Africans measured distance by the number of days it would take to walk it. A few more people approached our car. To them, Dad seemed friendly, and they too grinned sheepishly. I spoke to a man who told me, *"Barabara yote nafika Malindi"* (All roads lead to Malindi). The forks in the road rejoined one another, and the diversions were there only to avoid muddy patches during rainy seasons.

We waved *kwaheri* (goodbye) and Dad drove on. We arrived at our hotel at about 4:00am. The hotel owner was awakened and showed us to our room. We slept until 8:00, had breakfast, and left for the salt pans a few miles further northwards. We arrived at a large corrugated iron building that housed a refinery and bagging equipment. Three Africans came out to tell us their employer was waiting for us down at the salt pans. They ushered us to a light, narrow-gauge rail trolley, and we set off with one man standing on a platform behind us and two men pushing at a run. They ran bare foot along the top of the sun heated steel rails which were no more than an inch wide. What their feet were made of, I can't imagine. They ran cheerfully for about three miles, taking turns to rest on the platform. We arrived at the salt pans to meet the Indian owner of the company. While Dad went to talk business, I had a look at the operation.

At high tides, the sea was allowed to enter the pans through removable wooden gates. The pans were areas thirty feet square bounded on four sides by a ten-inch-high mud wall. As the tide began to ebb, gates in the seaward walls were closed to retain the seawater in the pans from which the sun evaporated the water to leave the salt. After several tides, there was enough salt to begin raking it into piles for transportation to the refinery and bagging.

The process was simple but slow, and was not unlike the collection of soda ash at Magadi. I have doubts as to the commercial viability of the venture which may have been a pilot scheme, but forty years later salt was still being produced there.

As we returned to the refinery, our three stalwarts were chatting among themselves as they pushed the trolley at a steady run. One asked Dad if he had ever worked at Magadi. Dad said he had, some fifteen years earlier. It turned out all three men had been employed at Magadi eighteen years previously, and remembered Dad. They were of the Luo tribe from western Kenya. Dad had found the Luos the most productive at Magadi. They received handsome gratuities from Dad for having pushed us a total distance of about six miles through the heat and humidity of the day along too-hot-to touch steel rails.

7

Swimmin' and Surfin'

All along the Kenya coast, about 300 yards from the beach, there is a reef which is largely exposed at low tide when the water between the beach and the reef is shallow, and is warmed by the sun. There are no sharks in the shallows as it is cut off from the deeper water by the reef. As the tide rises, there is a strong current that runs parallel to the beach, and this current enables a swimmer to cover a surprising distance without tiring, and without wavelets splashing into his face.

In his school-days, Dad became a strong swimmer and in my childhood, he taught me to swim. In my early teens, he and I went 'cruising'. Mum drove us some miles down the coast. Dad and I entered the water and swam leisurely with the current, back to base. This could take several hours. If we tired, we swam to the shore to rest, but that was seldom necessary. I found that I could change from crawl to side stroke to enable me to 'rest'. I enjoyed the comradeship of these swims with Dad although we were each alone with our own thoughts. There was, nevertheless, a sense of a shared experience, as well as a feeling of achievement.

***

When I reached the age of twelve we took our annual August holiday at Malindi. In those days Malindi was famous for its surfing. There is a pass through the reef and big rollers came surging towards the beach to break 100 yards out and race over the intervening water to wash high up on the beach. At full spring tide these waves were enormous, and not everyone could manage them. But there was a line of secondary waves which broke in about five feet of water and were big enough to surf on without the problem of having to swim out to catch the big waves in deep water.

We surfed lying on plywood boards, and I had to swim with mine out to the big breakers through the constant rush of waves racing toward the beach. The enormous undertow as breakers rushed seaward again was a hazard to be taken on only by strong swimmer. By the time I was twelve, I could enjoy this sport.

However, I became a little too confident. At low tide the rollers broke in shallow water, almost on the beach. Mum and Dad and sisters, Elizabeth and Margaret, were sitting on the veranda of our hotel chalet when I marched down onto the beach with my surfboard. The tide was on the ebb but the breakers were surprisingly big. I decided to ride a few waves. I became absorbed, and didn't notice that, as the tide reached its lowest point, the breakers were crashing down on the beach.

Suddenly I was swept off my feet by the undertow, and dragged under sand-laden water to a huge breaker that smashed me onto the hard sand of the almost exposed beach. I was carried up the beach rolling over and over in the surf. I'd lost my board. My mouth, ears, eyes and hair were full of sand. I tried to regain my feet, but was dragged back by the strong undertow of a receding wave, and was overcome by the next breaker. I was picked up and smashed down again, this time upside-down on my neck. Now I was stunned as well as blinded by sand. The sea had me in its grip, and played with me as though I were a rag doll in the mouth of a playful dog.

Time and time again I tried to regain my feet or drag myself out of the water on hands and knees, but to no avail. I didn't panic, realising that I must try to keep my head, or not survive the ordeal. I was becoming drained of my strength when a huge wave picked me up. I took a deep breath but only succeeded in taking in water before being driven to the bottom with such force that I had the wind knocked out of me. Knowing that I would not be able to withstand further punishment, I made ready for one last effort.

I was carried by the surf towards the shore, and for an instant I saw Mum running toward me. She was not a strong swimmer, and it was imperative that I got into shallow water or she would find herself in the same dangerous predicament. With a Herculean effort, I managed to get out of the undertow, and crawled on hands and knees to Mum, and collapsed in shallow water. My legs were trembling as Mum helped me up onto the beach. Dad, believing that I could handle any situation in the water, hadn't realised the power of the breakers, and only decided to come down from the chalet when he saw me crawl from the water. I was too exhausted to speak, but Mum knew the terror I'd been in, and sat beside me as I gasped for air.

Dad arrived and stood beside me. Sympathetically he said, "You've had a narrow escape, old soldier. Come with me," and he grasped my arm and ushered me towards the water.

"I'll never go in the water again." I gasped, still unable to breathe normally.

"You'll be all right with me," Dad assured me, and a few moments later I found myself chest deep in a small breaker on which I body surfed up onto the beach. Dad was grinning and called me back. He had recovered my surfboard and had his own. Together we surfed in on another small wave. As Dad would have said, I was back in the saddle again.

Gogglin' (later known as snorkelin' and scuba divin')

During one vacation when the whole family was at Malindi, I had a magical experience. I was thirteen and could swim like a fish. The wonder of tropical waters is in their clarity. Scenes are breathtaking when the sun shines down through clear water to strike the brilliantly colored fishes, corals and plant growth. Dad had told me about a glass bottomed boat in which he had taken a trip near Port Said in the Suez Canal. He had seen a myriad of tiny iridescent fish, colorful coral and beautiful seaweed.

It was then 1944, and underwater swimming was without goggles or face masks, so everything was blurred. In those days we never saw color films of underwater life, and any fish caught at sea by the local fishermen very quickly lost their color. By the time a catch was brought to shore, it was usually rather drab.

Staying at our hotel was a friend of my parents, Howard Stent. One evening, while we were having dinner, he rushed up to Dad and asked if he had ever been goggling. Dad said he hadn't, and Howard said he'd been out that day. He insisted Dad go with him the following day, and suggested that I go too.

With Howard, we boarded a 12-foot sailboat. The captain of our craft was a local fisherman employed by the hotel. He was a small, lean man with a crinkled black face. He had a wonderful grin which wrinkled the crows' feet around his bright brown eyes. He wore a colorful *kikoi* (sarong) secured by a leather belt from which hung a sheathed knife. A loosely tied matching turban led me to suppose that he was a Muslim, as many Africans along the East African coast follow the Islamic tenets. He wore no shoes on his gnarled feet which we were to discover could walk over sharp coral or across the burning sand of the exposed beach without detriment.

We sailed out to a gap in the reef and then turned to sail parallel to it on the seaward side. The tide was high and the wind was against us, and I learned a little about tacking against the wind - in particular to duck when the captain yelled "Going about" and the boom came over to deal a memorable blow to those who ignored him.

I quickly realised that our captain was a very skilled and experienced sailor. He took us to a place between two spur reefs that projected out to sea from the shore, and threw out the anchor in quite shallow, absolutely calm, clear water. He distributed face masks, explained how to adjust them, and how to ensure they didn't fog by spitting into them and smearing the spittle on the glass. We then climbed overboard into three feet of water, bent down and found that we were on the edge of a thirty foot deep submarine cliff.

I was overwhelmed by the sheer beauty of the scene. Never had I expected to see such color. I had to raise my head to gasp. I found Dad doing the same. We were completely dumbstruck. Down we bent again, and gazed at the scene until we could hold our breath no longer. We had no snorkels or flippers. We wore shorts and tennis shoes, which were cumbersome in the water. We found that we could lie on the surface and look down onto a wonderful variety of fish of all sizes, shapes and colors. There were many varieties of colorful coral through which all manner of seaweed grew.

I found that by slowly expelling the breath from my lungs, I could sink down the cliff side to look into holes and caves to see yet more fish. As I sank deeper, the fish got bigger but less colorful. We spent several hours there, and I later heard that Dad and Howard had spent a lot of time watching me. Seemingly I was as interesting to watch as the fish as I descended slowly through thirty feet of water to the bottom of the cliff. I discovered if I lay inert in the water, I could stay down for nearly three minutes without difficulty. Dad and Howard timed several of my underwater descents. I have never forgotten that first experience of goggling, and the wondrous feelings.

The captain had been urging us to climb aboard for some time. The tide was ebbing, and our way home was jeopardized because the reefs were becoming exposed. We then learned just how skilled our captain was. We arrived at the uncovered reef. Our captain turned the yacht side-on to the reef, lowered the sail and raised the centerboard. I was given the job of hauling the sail up as fast as I could on the captain's word of command.

As a large wave approached, I received the order, and the sail shot up. The captain was at the helm, and the boat spun round. The wind filled the sail and the wave caught the yacht and carried us over the reef in a rush. Our captain's timing was perfect. We had 'surfed' to the other side of the reef on the crest of the wave without a scratch. We sailed quietly back to the landing beach where our gallant captain was thanked, and rewarded handsomely for taking us on such a magical adventure.

When I went back to school after that holiday, we were told to write an essay on 'A day in the Holidays'. I wrote about that day when I'd been overwhelmed by the beauty of underwater life. My essay was apparently good enough to be read out to the class. Twenty-seven years later, I was working in my office when I heard my secretary speaking to someone. She came in to say a Mr. Fox wished to see me, and I asked her to show him in. Jim Fox peered round the door, grinned and cried out, "I knew it must be you". He came in and sat down and said, "You are the guy who wrote that essay about goggling, aren't you?" Jim had been in the same class with me at school. I was quite flattered that someone had remembered my essay for so long.

***

I built up stamina and, when I was about fifteen, I swam round Mombasa Island from one side of Makupa Causeway, to the other. Not only was this quite an achievement, it was also quite a dangerous escapade, as there were two sections where it was regularly frequented by sharks. This swim was done as a challenge. I'd met an Italian PoW who had been watching me swim.

Although a PoW, he seemed to have a large measure of freedom. He suggested that I enter the water as the tide was on the ebb so that a current would draw me along the Tudor creek, past a slaughterhouse, a shark infested area. At a later part of the swim, the rising tide would help propel me through Kilindini Harbour past the ships, in another shark area, to the other side of the causeway. As I remember, the swim took me about seven hours. I emerged tired but satisfied with my achievement.

My great regret was that I failed to take the name of my Italian pal, who watched my progress round the island from various vantage points. As a PoW, there were areas that were out of bounds to him, but I was sure, had I got into trouble, he would have come to my aid. He seemed to be as happy as I, that I had managed the swim.

He told me he had been attending Perugia University when he was conscripted into the Italian military and assigned to submarine duties. He had been one of several frogmen who had disembarked from a submarine to take up residence in a wreck lying off-shore, from which he and his colleagues made raids into Gibraltar Harbor, attaching limpet mines to British warships to blow them up. His wartime experiences had been tremendously exciting, and he felt himself very lucky, not only to have survived, but to have been sent to Kenya for internment. He was, however, desperate for the war to end, so that he could get back to his family, girlfriend and his studies.

***

I was again on holiday at Malindi when I met up with Peter, an older school friend. He had been asked to deal with some mamba (crocodile) that had come down the Sabaki River, and had taken up residence in tidal waters.

Two women villagers had disappeared as they washed their families' clothes, and the crocs had taken a number of cattle as they drank from the river.

The local Game Warden was absent in hospital, and Peter had agreed to try to shoot some of the crocs. But a scantily clad, lissome young maiden had engaged his attention, and so he asked me to deal with the crocs. He handed me an old 8mm Mannlicher rifle in very good condition and a couple of handfuls of hard-nosed ammo. His scantily clad maiden spared him long enough to drive up to the river where he left me, promising to come back at about 6.00 pm

I wandered upstream for a few hundred yards to the village that had suffered from the croc depredations. The villagers told me that this was the place the crocs congregated. I walked a few yards further and settled down into a comfortable position on a grassy bank overlooking the river, from where I could cover a couple of hundred yards in each direction .

I didn't have to wait for long before a croc stuck his eyes and nose above the water. I took careful aim and squeezed the trigger. The croc reared up, fell back into the shallow water and disappeared. In no time another croc appeared with the same results. This was repeated again and again and again. I lost count but thought I'd rid the area of about thirteen man-eaters. What had happened to the dead crocs, I didn't know, other than they each had taken an 8mm bullet as close to the eye as I could place it. I knew that every shot had found its mark, not only from the reaction of each croc, but also from the unmistakable sound of a bullet hitting its target

As evening approached, I went to meet Peter, who arrived looking very tired but happy. I told him of my day, and he said that it is very difficult to recover dead crocs, which seem always to manage to die in the river to be washed downstream. This proved to be true, as over the next couple of days the carcasses of twelve dead crocs washed up on the Malindi beach.

My popularity amongst the hoteliers was questionable, but the villagers were much more enthusiastic, and asked me back so that they could ceremoniously present me with a Walungulu bow and arrows, which the Game Warden confiscated on his return from hospital. Nobody was supposed to have a poacher's weapon. And while the hoteliers didn't want dead crocs turning up on the beach, the hotel guests thought I was a great hunter, and bought me a bottle of pop whenever I hit the bar. Any remaining crocs were sensible enough to move upstream, and no more people or cattle were taken.

8

Circumcision

Circumcision is an important ritual amongst Africans. The ritual differs from tribe to tribe but there are some common elements. The number seven has significance in many tribes, and a child is said to have been born, not in a year, but within a seven-year period. Each seven-year period has a name, and this is given as the birth date. As an example, let us say a seven-year period called *Mtini* (fig tree) began in 1951, it ended in 1957. A person born in that seven-year period, when asked his or her birth date, would reply "*Mtini*". During the next seven-year period a *Mtini* child is expected to begin to help with family, farming and tribal chores such as herding cattle, planting, weeding and harvesting, feeding the chickens, and collecting the eggs By the end of the second seven-year period the *Mtini* child will be between its eighth and fourteenth year. It is during the third seven year-period that the *Mtini* child faces the circumcision ordeal.

In the case of male children, a lad is to pass from boyhood to manhood, and is expected to show the utmost indifference to pain. In this he is helped in various ways. One tribe has the boys stand in a river during the night so that cold water numbs their willies - they hope. Another tribe has the lads run a gauntlet naked, between two lines of warriors lashing at willies with stinging nettles. The aim is to so sting the wrinkled retainers that the amputation passes unnoticed - they hope.

After undergoing the numbing or stinging exercise, the boys are lined up and an assistant draws their foreskins forward, and pushes thorns through to prevent them from shrinking back. The *Mganga* (medicine man) then goes down the line severing foreskins with a piece of sharp flint, obsidian glass, knife, panga or whatever comes to hand. During this procedure the tenderfoot warrior is not supposed to flinch or say "Ouch!" Having successfully endured the ordeal, he is regarded as having reached manhood. Should he fail to pass the test and cry out in pain, the boy will be regarded, forevermore, as an unmanly weakling to be scorned by all his tribe.

The next seven year period will see him become a tribal warrior, and for the succeeding seven years he is regarded as an elder under tribal headmen and the chief. Prior to the colonization of Kenya by the Brits, Africans did not expect to live much beyond the age of thirty-five. They died, not from old age, but from attacks by wild animals, tribal warfare, disease and curses put upon them by the *Mchawi* (witch doctor) for having upset a comrade by encroaching on his land, stealing his livestock or some other perceived transgression.

No Good Deed.......

During one term at the PoW a whooping cough epidemic broke out. All the day-boys were asked to stay at home, and remain there in quarantine. I had to stay away from school. My classmate, Peter Beckley, who lived 400 yards from our house, also had to stay at home. Peter, small and sickly, was a serious asthmatic. For him to catch whooping cough would have been dangerously prostrating.

Mrs. Beckley had been a school teacher, and it was agreed that Peter and I study under her tutoring. Normally a motherly woman, she could also be strict, and she was insistent that her son and I did several hours of study each day. Together the three of us managed to cover the term's syllabus very satisfactorily with Mrs. Beckley being particularly helpful in French, mathematics and geography, which she had taught at a high school in England before coming to Kenya.

I walked to Peter's home each day, carrying a load of the books I would need. One day, as I walked to Peter's, I heard a child screaming in terror. I ran forward to a bus terminus, a half circle of asphalt to one side of the road, where buses could turn round for their return to Nairobi's center. Round the edge of the terminus, a shallow, open, storm-drain channeled rain from the asphalt. Beyond the drain I saw three African men crouching round a four-year old European boy who was screaming in terror. The three men had taken the boy's shorts down, and were examining his little penis. This was an unheard of invasion of a child's privacy by adult Africans. Normally they were extraordinarily kind, considerate and protective of children.

I charged the group, rage preventing any thought of prudence. The two men on either side of the little boy saw me coming, jumped to their feet and ran off. The little boy pulled up his pants, mounted his tricycle, and sped off up the road. The man squatting with his back to me received the toe of my tennis shoe painfully, and just as hard as I could kick. I jerked to a halt. The man stood up, and turned toward me. He had his right hand to his back, and I wondered if my kick had jolted a kidney or two out of place. His hand appeared gripping a knife with a glittering nine inch long blade. He lunged at me, and in doing so, stepped in the shallow storm-drain. Attempting to regain his balance, he stumbled forward with his neck outstretched, arms flailing. I stepped aside, and as he passed me, I punched him hard on the side of his neck. That punch, delivered with desperation,

77

had all my weight behind it. I was determined to end the attack instantly as I was unwilling to get entangled with a furious thirty-year-old adult. His knife jabbed into my left thigh, but the gash was not deep as the stab was delivered by a wildly flailing arm, not a deliberate thrust.

He went down face first into the gravel, as though pole-axed. I left the scene with whatever dignity I could muster. I hastened to Peter's house with blood running down my leg into my shoe, hoping that I appeared to be hurrying because I was late, and not because I was fearful of another confrontation with a knife-wielding, angry adult. Mrs. Beckley washed my jagged wound, and covered it with a sticking plaster. She phoned the police who came to take a statement before setting out to look for a man with a stiff neck and a swollen, grazed face. We heard no more about the incident.

On reflection, I suspect that the three men had heard that some European males were circumcised shortly after birth, were curious to see if this was true, and were intrigued to find out the extent of the operation. Many Kenya-born European male infants were routinely circumcised for hygienic reasons in Africa's hot, dusty environment.

Hardened Delinquents

We had a couple of refugees from war-torn Europe at the PoW School. They arrived in 1946 or 1947 shortly after the end of the war. One, Jacob, had been a prisoner in one of Hitler's death camps. Jacob had survived, but suffered mentally and emotionally, and it was very difficult to know how to treat him. He was an inveterate thief. Although there was no reason for him to steal from other boys, as he had much the same possessions as everyone else, he couldn't help himself. And while his victims were usually understanding, and were prepared to forgive him if they got their possessions back, there came a time when patience

78

wore thin. I took an interest in Jacob, and I thought that he felt he could trust me, and look on me as a friend. One lad had unlocked his locker, and then rushed to the bathroom for a few moments. On his return he found Jacob helping himself from his locker. Although caught red-handed, Jacob denied the offense. I was then a prefect, and the victim reported the matter to me, knowing that I had befriended the unfortunate refugee.

I had a few words with Jacob, and asked him how he would feel if someone stole from him. He seemed very contrite, and I suggested that, if he felt moved to steal again, he should come to me, and we would talk about it. I hoped he might feel that I was someone with whom he could talk over his problem, and he seemed to think that the idea might help. But a few days later another boy was robbed, and Jacob was automatically suspected. I was called, and asked Jacob to empty his pockets and open his locker. Quantities of loot were found, and I told Jacob that I would now have to report the matter to the House-master, Mr. Stewart. Jacob had, up to this point, been treated with kid gloves, and when I asked him to accompany me to the House-master, he readily agreed. I knocked on Mr Stewart's door, and when he opened the door and saw who it was, he looked stern.

"What is it?" he asked.

"I'd like a word with you about Jacob, Sir," I said.

"Come in," he invited. "No," he said to Jacob, "you wait there."

I told Mr Stewart of the events in which I had been involved with Jacob, and Mr Stewart made a few notes. He then told me I could leave, and invited Jacob in. I never saw Jacob again, but heard that he had been seen packing his possessions. What happened to him, I don't know, and I was rather disappointed by the fact that we hadn't been able to handle his problem more effectively.

***

Another refugee, who got into much more serious trouble, was Hans Prater. He and his parents had also suffered at the hands of the Nazis. Prater came to the PoW when he was about 14. He was fairly tall, thin and had a hunted look. He was forever glancing about, looking over his shoulder but avoiding eye contact. Every morning at 8:00am all Christians had to attend Assembly. Prayers were said, a lesson read, and the Headmaster would give a few words of spiritual guidance. This was followed by a hymn. After our Christian devotions were over, the Headmaster made daily announcements. The non-Christians did not have to attend Assembly, but were expected to have their own meeting under a senior boy of their own faith, and Prater attended the Jewish gathering.

One day the Headmaster announced that the practice of writing or drawing on the chalkboards during the mid-morning break was to cease. His talk reminded me that this was quite an absorbing pastime, so the following break saw me drawing on a chalkboard - not in my own classroom, of course, but in another where my art was less well known. Prater was drawing at the other end of the 12 ft chalkboard.

When the bell rang announcing the end of the break period, I grabbed the chalkboard eraser, and started to wipe out my masterpiece. Prater demanded the eraser, and I said "Hang on a minute. I'm nearly finished with it." Prater came over and kicked me on the shin. This was a silly thing to do. I was taller, heavier and stronger than he. I turned and hit Prater heavily on the chest - not wanting to hurt my fist on his head. Prater took off backwards, and didn't stop until he hit the far wall, where he slid down in a somewhat stunned state. I finished wiping the chalkboard, and went to my own classroom.

We were well into a Latin lesson, when a boy came in and spoke to our Latin master, who told me the Headmaster wanted to see me, immediately. I found Prater in the Head's office, the Head looking a little irritated. He told Prater to wait outside his office, and asked me for my version of what had happened. I told him. I didn't actually accuse the Head for reminding me what fun it is to draw on the chalkboard during the break, but I did let him know that, had he not raised the subject, I might not have been tempted.

He gave me four over the tail with a cane, and told me to wait outside. He called Prater in, telling him to leave the door open. He told Prater that he too had broken a school rule about drawing on the chalkboard but, in addition, he had been churlish and had assaulted me. Furthermore he had snitched on me, and this demanded a more severe punishment. Prater was given six over the tail, and came out sobbing. He rushed off to complain to his father, who was the piano teacher at the school.

Prater became a member of a gang of nine to fifteen year-old boys. He was a day-boy, a 'Stinker'. Another 'Stinker', one of the older boys, was the gang leader. They had built a tree-house in a wood in a residential area, which was the target of attacks by a rival gang, firing air rifles. I never heard of any boy being hurt in exchanges of air rifle pellets. But there came a time when, somehow, some gang members armed themselves with pistols and revolvers. Prater managed to get his hands on a Colt .45 semi-automatic pistol and some ammunition.

One day the Headmaster called me to his office. He told me that a new boy was to come to the school the following day, and asked me to show the boy around the school. I met Ray, the son of a senior officer who was a padre in the Royal Air Force. Ray seemed a quiet, well behaved lad. His black, wiry hair suggested vitality and his twinkling dark brown eyes bespoke cheerfulness. He was a day-boy, and lived with his parents in the same residential hotel as the Prater family. I showed Ray to his classroom, to the toilets and to the locker room. At lunch time I took him to the dining room, and I also showed him where the sports fields were, and generally made sure that he knew where to go and at what time. For the next few days I made sure that Ray fitted into the routine.

Six weeks after our first meeting, I was distressed when asked to be one of six schoolboy pall-bearers at Ray's funeral. Prater had shot and killed him. This was the first funeral I had attended. Ray's parents stood at the graveside, his father in full dress uniform. Mrs. Ray, grieving deeply, was supported on the arm of her husband, who showed great restraint and dignity. After we had lowered the coffin into the grave, the attending padre said the words "Dust to dust, ashes to ashes," and bent to pick up a handful of earth which he scattered into the grave. The earth contained several pebbles and these hit the coffin with a dreadful, irreverent racket. Overcome by grief, Ray's mother collapsed to her knees, almost bringing down her mortified husband.

The rest of the little graveside service went by unheard as several mourners tried to help Ray's parents. After the service was over, we six schoolboy pall-bearers went over to the school bus, and waited to be driven back to school. After a few minutes, Ray's father came over to us, but he was overcome with grief and was only able to choke out a single word, "Thanks". We returned to school crushed by the realization of the extent to which the waste of a young life saddened those who loved him.

After the funeral, it was learned that Prater used to bring his Colt to school, and stick up his fellow Jews at their morning gathering. While he was treated as a bit of a joke, the boys used to put their hands up, as Prater had shown extreme rage when anyone told him to sod off, which might have led to their own funeral.

My family's doctor had been the first medical practitioner to be called to the hotel where Ray's body lay on the bed in Prater's bedroom. The doctor had found no bullet holes in the shirt that Ray was wearing. The slug had entered low on his left side, and had passed upwards diagonally through his body towards his right shoulder. Prater's story was that the two boys had been talking in his room, and Ray had picked up the Colt and pointed it at Prater. He had told Ray that it was a dangerous thing to do, and had tried to take the pistol away from Ray. A struggle ensued, and the gun went off, killing Ray. Prater denied that he had put Ray's shirt on his corpse. The doctor gave evidence at Prater's trial, and said that it would take a very strong man to have twisted Ray's right arm, with the gun in his hand, into the position from which the bullet entered the body and passed through to the shoulder on the other side of the body. In fact, Ray's shoulder would have to have been torn out of joint.

Despite the doctor's evidence, and that of the boys who had been held at gun point by Prater on numerous occasions, Prater was found not guilty. The judge couldn't reverse the jury's verdict, but he clearly disagreed with it and said so. He gave Mr. Prater three months to remove his son from Kenya. After the family left, I never heard of them again, but I wondered how Prater's parents felt at the shame and disgrace their wretched son had brought upon them.

Effects of Nazi Experimentation

My chum, Harry MacDonald, had to have an operation to sew up a hernia. I and several friends used to visit our pal in hospital as he always seemed to have a good stock of grapes, which we enjoyed.

In the hospital at the same time was a sixteen-year old Polish Jew, who had been subjected to frightful experiments by the Nazis. His legs and lower torso had been frozen. Why he had been sent to Kenya, I don't know. The Nazi experiments had started when the boy was about nine. He was under constant treatment for pain, and by the time I met him, morphine was having little effect. The only English the boy knew was the word 'pain'. He constantly cried out "Pain. Pain. Pain." Nurses knew the lad was an addict, and gave him injections in strict accordance with doctor's instructions. I had sat by his bed, and had offered him grapes, but he was withdrawn into the misery of his suffering, and turned away, seeking lonely isolation.

One day I drove several grape-eaters to visit Harry, who was soon to be released from hospital. For some reason I had to return to the car, while the rest of my pals went on ahead to get at the grapes. The entrance to the wards was through swing doors. As I approached them, they opened to allow a tall, gaunt man to exit. He was dressed in khaki trousers, a cotton shirt and laced leather boots. I took him for an Afrikaner farmer, and this was confirmed when he spoke to me in a heavy South African accent.

"Have you met that poor Polish boy?" he asked.

"Yes," I replied. "He suffers unbearable pain."

The farmer told me that he had come down from Eldoret, where there was quite a large Afrikaner community. He had an orchard where he grew several different types of fruit, and once a month came down to Nairobi for supplies, and brought with him a few sacks of fruit, which he delivered free to the hospital for the patients.

"Do you know," he continued, speaking very slowly, "twenty-seven years ago my wife died suddenly, and I was struck dumb. I have just been told what happened to that Polish boy. You are the first person to whom I have been able to speak since my wife died." I was too stupefied to reply, and the Afrikaner slowly walked away. He was stunned by the miracle that had returned his power of speech. I joined my grape-eating friends, but it was some minutes before I could break my silence to tell them what had just happened. We were all hushed, and none of us felt inclined to eat any more grapes. We left the hospital agreeing that from all events some good emerges. The Afrikaner's years of silence had ended. I heard a few weeks later that the Polish boy finally found painless peace when he passed away.

9

The Treat's on Who? Ben Hur?

One afternoon I was in town with three friends, and we decided to go to a popular restaurant. We were all about fifteen and had energy to spare. The Horseshoe Restaurant was owned by the parents of one of our school friends, and we expected generous treatment. We had tea and sandwiches, and waited for the check. It didn't come. We chatted happily, and forgot about the bill.

After a couple of hours, we left the restaurant, and wandered down Government Road, one of Nairobi's main streets, to peer into shop windows. As we stood outside a sports shop a rickshaw passed by and, in a flash, we were hurrying down to the bus terminus from where it was also possible to hire rickshaws. By the time we arrived there it was getting dark, and the rickshaw operators had gone home. We grabbed a rickshaw and, with two of us towing, and the other two as passengers, we sped off. We raced our chariot round the now traffic-free town center, hurtling round corners flat out. As one pair tired, the passengers took over, and Nairobi's town center was filled with gleeful shouts and laughter - until a cop car, with siren wailing, arrived on the scene.

We had raced past the Horseshoe Restaurant several times, where a waiter had reported our failure to pay for our meal. He had informed the restaurant manager, who had phoned the police. After returning the rickshaw, we were escorted back to the Horseshoe.

As regards the unpaid check, we claimed that we had forgotten to pay and, in part, this was the fault of the waiter, as he had evidently forgotten to present the check until he saw us terrorising the township by the dangerous operation of a rickshaw. The policeman was inclined to believe that the waiter had been dilatory, and the waiter agreed that, indeed, he had been remiss. We paid the bill.

As regards our chariot racing, the policeman seemed to think our misdeed was more a prank than a serious offense. He delivered a verbal reprimand, and sent us on our way. We dispersed gratified, with the thought that the policeman was a very understanding man. He had elicited a promise from us that we would never misbehave again, and we honored this pledge - at least as far as the town center was concerned.

Prehensile toes.

When we were about fifteen, one of my friends, Paul Wood, had very useful, exceptionally long, prehensile toes. He seemed quite fearless of heights. This enabled him to climb trees that none of the rest of us would dare tackle. A couple of the lads were birds' egg collectors, and Paul could always be persuaded to climb the most difficult trees to get eggs. One collector needed the egg of a black shouldered kite. A nest had been spotted in the highest branches of a giant blue-gum eucalyptus tree, and one day we decided that Paul should climb this tree while the rest of us hung about keeping watch. It was a real challenge as the tree was very tall and blue-gums have smooth, slippery bark. Paul gleefully accepted the challenge. He was a mite daft, and was ever

86

keen to show off his expertise and nerve, and he shinned up the tree with amazing alacrity.

The tree was in a coffee plantation, and we had determined that the farmhouse, which was only 300 feet from where we were keeping watch, was empty. Presumably the Jex-Blakes, who owned the property, were out. But suddenly Lady Jex-Blake appeared from the farmhouse striding down the lawn, fists clenched, and looking more than a little threatening

"What are you boys doing on my property?" she yelled.

I went into groveling mode and in the most polite terms whined, "We only wanted to climb this tree."

I pointed to a highly climbable tree a few yards to our right and in the opposite direction from the blue-gum.

"Well you should have asked my permission," said Lady J-B, slightly mollified by my fawning - I spoke with the best upper-class accent of which my mother approved.

"We did intend to ask, but the house seemed empty," I replied obsequiously.

My demeanor seemed to impress Lady J-B, who perhaps hadn't expected a gang of hooligans to be courteous.

"All right," decided Lady J-B, "but you mustn't climb higher than the lowest branches, and you must take great care. I don't want any of you falling out of the tree and hurting yourselves.

"Oh. Thank you so much," I said, "you're a such a good sport. Thank you so much," I groveled.

I had heard some of my friends choking back guffaws, but I had also heard a black shouldered kite attacking Paul, who had continued to climb towards the nest. At a height of about 150 ft, being attacked by an irate kite is not much fun. Nobody else seemed to hear the attacking kite. Had Lady J-B seen Paul so high up in the blue-gum, she might have suffered a heart attack but, after a few more words of admonishment, and an instruction to report to her when we left, she turned and strode back to the house.

I was heavily censured by my friends for having been such an obsequious little bootlicker, but I threatened them with violence. We climbed into the lower branches of the approved tree, and shouted gleefully to each other. This was to cover the sound of the wretched kites, and to distract attention from Paul, who was now climbing down the blue-gum with a kite's egg in his mouth so that he could use both hands, as well as all his prehensile toes to effect the descent. He finally reached the ground, and joined us as we scrambled down from the climbable tree. I was appointed spokesman to go and report our departure, which I did with great politeness and effusive thanks. I hastily turned to make my get-away.

"Come here, boy," shouted Lady J-B. "Who are you? What's your name?"

"Tom Sawyer," I yelled as I ran down to my waiting friends.

I didn't want Lady J-B making enquiries, finding my parent's phone number, and possibly inviting that nice, polite boy to tea or some other dreadful event. I didn't know anybody called Tom Sawyer, but had read about his Adventures, and had been impressed enough to think that the name might throw Lady J-B for long enough to say to herself, "I know that name," before she realised that we had conned her, and had really been up to some mischief. Paul got little attention despite his heroism, but I was the object of further derision until I again threatened violence. We trotted homewards, giggling joyfully at the success of our mission.

Pecker's Marital Adventures

Paul had an older brother, Pecker, who, like Paul, was an intrepid character. He was popular, but we saw little of him. We were still at school, but he had left and lived in a somewhat primitive, isolated dwelling in his employer's workshop compound some fifteen miles from Nairobi. We were surprised when he announced that he was going on six months 'home leave' to Britain, as he had never been there before, and had never indicated any wish to visit the Land of the Limies as we called our mother country. We were even more surprised when he told us he intended to get married. He had never shown any inclination to settle down, and we were unaware that any particular girl had successfully snared Pecker. He was well paid, good looking, strongly built, fair haired, blue eyed and had a terrific personality, and there was certainly no shortage of female admirers.

"Who are you going to marry?" we asked.

"Oh, I don't know. I haven't met anyone yet," he replied disinterestedly. "I guess I'll pick up a bird in the UK."

Well, that is exactly what he did. He arrived back with a super looking, intelligent, cheerful English girl, Mary, who was devoted to Pecker - and he to her. The wedding took place a little later, and Pecker and his bride went off to Pecker's mud-and-wattle, thatched rondavel. Pecker lived a simple life, and his accommodation was, as far as he was concerned, adequate. His bride seemed happy enough. If it was OK by Pecker, it was OK by her. According to Mary, they went to bed, and the following morning she felt Pecker slowly sliding out of bed. She smiled to herself. Her darling husband was clearly trying to get up without awakening her. But suddenly the blankets were torn off her, and she was unceremoniously yanked from the bed.

"Ha, ha! Caveman stuff," Mary thought, but then saw Pecker staring at the bed in horror. She looked down to see a large, thick snake staring at her with glassy eyes.

Pecker dealt with the still somnolent *pili* (puff-adder) with alacrity. He grabbed its tail and swung its head against a wall, stunning it. He was then able to knock its brains out with a *rungu* (club), which he kept by his bedside. He was far more worried by the presence of the deadly puff-adder than was his bride, who had every confidence in her wonderful husband who knew all about the wild creatures of Africa. Pecker thought it about time to move into a proper house that would be *pili* proof.

10

The Double Cross

When I was about fourteen, I learned just how unfeeling girls are. Elizabeth had made friends with a lovely, raven haired beauty named Anita, and soon her family, the Cross-Crosses, and ours became friends. Colonel Cross-Crosse had been an aide-de-camp to the Governor of Uganda. He was tall, slim, had a military bearing, and tended to shout at everybody. Mrs. C-C (aka Mrs. Criss-Cross or Mrs. Double-Cross) had a dignified and assured manner. They came to live in Kenya, and the Colonel changed the family name from Cross-Crosse to Cross-Upcott, which he considered to be a major improvement. But few friends used the new name, preferring the nicknames with which they were familiar. Anita and her younger sister, Gail, were frequent visitors to our house.

Gail was a precocious child, and was quite confident when dealing with adults. One Saturday afternoon the Col. took his family into the Nairobi Game Park where he managed to get his car stuck. They finally managed to unstick the car, but arrived back home late, covered with mud. Guests were expected for drinks and supper. Gail was instructed to have a quick shower, get into her pajamas, dressing gown and slippers, and hurry downstairs to meet the guests. She was to welcome them into the lounge, show them the drinks cabinet, and invite them to help themselves. Meanwhile, the rest of the family would be getting themselves laundered and suitably attired.

All went well, and when the guests arrived they were met by a charming little five-year old, who had all the confidence of a young lady. And she looked so sweet and innocent in her woolly dressing-gown and bedroom slippers. She led the guests into the lounge, and pointed out the drinks cabinet.

"Please help yourselves to drinks," she invited them as instructed.

"Oh. I think we'll wait for your Mum and Dad to come down."

The guests sat down on the sofa, and Gail sat opposite them with her chin cupped in her hands. She stared at them unblinkingly. The guests grew embarrassed, and looked down to see if the had left any buttons undone, or if there were signs of a past meal visible on their clothes. Gail continued to stare at them. They looked down at themselves again and rechecked. Nothing. Finally the lady asked.

"Gail, you are staring at us. Is there something wrong?"

"Well, you don't look like fishes," she replied thoughtfully, still sitting chin cupped in her hands.

There was an embarrassed giggle from the guests and the lady asked, "Should we look like fishes?"

"Well," said Gail, "Mummy and Daddy say you drink like fishes."

**

Anita Crosse-Upcott was a truly beautiful girl. She was slender, had long, well groomed raven hair, and delicately sculptured features. Maybe her nose was just a little pointed,

but this defect only highlighted the perfection and beauty of her other features. She also had a sparkling personality which shone through her twinkling brown eyes.

She had a happy, humorous disposition and an elegant, cultivated charm. Or so it seemed to a certain awkward, would-be suitor.

Anita accompanied us on a holiday to Mombasa one year. She and Elizabeth were much involved in popular music. Mr. Sinatra was a favorite, and they spent most of each day in their hotel chalet playing Sinatra records on a wind-up record player. I was rather taken with the lovely Anita, though she was two years my senior, and was almost totally ignorant of my existence, Mr. Sinatra being the hot marvel of the moment.

I decided the time had come to intrude on that relationship, and went to their chalet. There were two steps up into the room where Elizabeth and Anita were sitting on their beds with the gramophone on a low table between them. I attempted a macho sort of entrance, and did a standing jump onto the first step, followed by another into the room. The doorway was low and my head hit the lintel with a solid thud. I fell between the beds at the feet of the girls, stunned.

"Why not take all of me?" sang Mr Sinatra

"Oh, Leonard," cried my ever-loving, exasperated sister, "You'll upset the record player!"

Taking into consideration that I was stunned, and had fallen heavily onto a cement floor, this reaction from Elizabeth might be termed inconsiderate and unthinking. But worse: Anita was giggling.

"Oh, you fool!" she gasped between giggles.

I slowly got to my feet and staggered to my room, stars circling my pounding head. I hadn't attracted Anita's attention in quite the way I had intended. My budding interest in girls suffered a relapse.

There is nothing like a dame.

The following year, Anita again accompanied us to the coast, this time to Malindi. I was struck down with a bad case of measles, and was confined to my room with the curtains closed to keep the strong sunshine from damaging my inflamed eyes. I felt pretty rough, and was disappointed in not being able to enjoy surfing on the big waves for which Malindi was famous.

My bedroom door opened, and Elizabeth and Anita entered. 'Oh,' I thought 'how nice of the girls to come to visit poor sick Leonard.'

"Can you lend me one of your white cotton shirts?" asked Anita. "We want to go surfing and I don't want to get sunburned." No, they were not being thoughtful and considerate. They just wanted to go and enjoy themselves while I, poor lad, lay on my sick-bed and nobody to chat with. I couldn't even read, as my eyes were too sore.

"Yeah. Sure. You'll find my shirts in the second drawer down," I said gallantly, despite my disappointment.

Anita dived into the drawer, found a suitable shirt, and the two girls rushed off without even closing the drawer. Are all girls so unthinking and inconsiderate, I wondered. They were back in fifteen minutes. Anita was trembling with rage.

"You rotten swine!" she screamed. "You might have warned me."

"About what?"

"You know perfectly well," she yelled.

"I don't. What is she on about?" I asked Elizabeth.

"Your shirt became see-through when wet. Anita wasn't wearing her bikini top," explained my sister.

I burst into fits of laughter. Well, hadn't Anita laughed at me when I fell at her feet, stunned and embarrassed? I could be unsympathetic too. Anita never really forgave me, but I think I saw a gleam of amusement in

Elizabeth's eye. My budding interest in girls suffered another relapse.

There IS nothing like a dame.

***

Mrs. Cross-Upcott was rather deaf. She adopted a method to avoid having to constantly ask people to repeat themselves. She would say "Fancy that!" which Mrs. Cross-Upcott thought was unlikely to be offensive, and if it was irrelevant, it was of little consequence. It might just draw the conclusion that Mrs. Cross-Upcott was becoming a little batty.

Mrs. Cross-Upcott went to have her hair done by her favorite hairdresser, Fabrizzio. She was accompanied by Anita who recounted the following story. Fabrizzio was always glad to see Mrs. Cross-Upcott, as she seemed so sympathetic. On this occasion he told his favorite customer of how he had recently learned of the death of his dear mother. He told her of the impecunious state that prevented his flying to Italy. He went on at length about how he hadn't been there to comfort his little sister, who had just suffered a loss when her husband ran off with the butcher's wife." ("Ran off with a butcher's knife?" Mrs. Cross-Upcott heard snatches of the tale). Now a second loss had overtaken his little sister, and he wasn't there to join his family in their grief. Hoping for a generous gratuity, Fabrizzio waxed lyrical about his own anguish.

Some members of his family wouldn't understand his absence from the funeral, and would ascribe it to indifference. His eldest brother - he had eight siblings - was the worst. Marco would have told everyone how Fabrizzio had always shown a lack of interest in his family, but this was completely untrue. None of his family had written to him to describe the burial, and he just knew that this was because Marco had poisoned their thoughts.

Who had attended the ceremony? Had Magda, another sister, managed to attend with her husband? Magda lived in America with her successful husband. Fabrizzio didn't even know the details of poor mama's death. It wouldn't have been right for an old lady of eighty-seven to have suffered. Poor Fabrizzio was so grieved that tears were streaming down his face. He couldn't go on with the sad story.

"Fancy that!" said Mrs. Cross-Upcott. Anita raised the back of her hand to her forehead in exasperated embarrassment.

11

A Long Walk

During my teens I enjoyed freedom to go hiking, hunting, and camping during school holidays. One adventure took place in 1947 when I was sixteen. A school friend, Bob, 6'4", slender, a fine athlete, and an outstanding student, suggested we take a 200 mile walk from Nairobi to Isiolo in the Northern Frontier District - and back. We planned to take very little money, and just a little canned meat to be eaten only in emergencies. We also took a change of clothing, but little else.

It was to be a test of endurance. We were to cover nearly 400 miles in about nine days, and did not intend to thumb lifts. Bob, I knew, had plenty of stamina as he was a fine miler, but I wondered if either of us could keep going for nine days at an average of nearly forty-five miles per day. We were to depend entirely on our youthful health, exuberance and staying power. Determination is all very well, but what if one of us became ill or suffered injury? Such thoughts were pushed aside by enthusiasm.

Bob came to my parent's house on his bicycle, and Mum gave us a lift to the start of our trek from the Muthaiga police station roundabout, two miles from our house and four miles from the center of Nairobi. The first day took us about thirty miles to Thika, where we slept the night at the home of a school friend, John Dodds. Although John was away, his parents saw to it that we were well fed, and we set off early the following morning on a forty-two mile march to the railway station at the little village of Sagana.

It became clear to me that Bob liked to walk beside me but about nine inches ahead. The more I tried to come alongside him, the faster he walked. So, I accepted his quirk, and we strode along at a good pace with Bob maintaining his lead. At Sagana, the Goan stationmaster fed us well, saying he enjoyed our company. Life for him as the only Goan in Sagana was lonely. He also gave us a room in which to sleep. We were now over seventy miles from Nairobi, and felt fit and energetic.

The following day we took leave from our kind host, and walked another twenty-eight miles or so to Nyeri, where we stayed with friends of Bob's father, who was supposed to have sent a telegram asking that we be given shelter. But the telegram hadn't arrived. Nevertheless, we enjoyed the hospitality of our hosts before setting out the next day on a shorter hike to Naro Moro. There we slept by the roadside. We awoke cold and hungry, opened a can of corned beef, and set off long before dawn on a forty-two mile trek to Timau.

We arrived there fourteen hours later, and were lucky to find our proposed hosts, Mr. and Mrs. 'Tiny' Gibbs, who were attending an after-match party at the local polo ground. Tiny, as one might expect, was a giant of a man, and his wife was petite. Tiny had been a gentleman's gentleman, and had inherited his employer's estate in Kenya. This included a farm and a magnificent mock Tudor mansion full of beautiful antique furniture, paintings, drawings, ornaments, crockery, glassware and cutlery. Again a telegram hadn't arrived from Bob's father asking Tiny and his wife to put us up, but again hospitality was lavish. We began to wonder if Bob's Dad had sent off the telegrams. Perhaps he had forgotten - or maybe he wanted to test our initiative.

Tiny's wife apologized profusely for the only accommodation she had available. This was a separate guest house with a lounge and library on the ground floor, a bathroom and an enormous bedroom upstairs. Mrs. Tiny also apologized for the beds, four-posters, the size of which was difficult to gauge from the bedroom doorway as they were far away across the spacious room.

We were very weary after our long walk and meager, early morning meal of half a can of beef each. We retired early after a light snack, and a luxurious bath. The following morning we found Mrs. Tiny cutting flowers in her splendid garden. We assured her that we had slept well, and then went in to sit down with Tiny to a huge breakfast of a choice of fruit, followed by scrambled eggs, bacon, sautéed kidneys, toast and marmalade, washed down with tea. We ate off fine bone china using heavy silver cutlery.

After a cheery farewell, we set off for Meru. This, again, was a hike of some forty miles. The road took us up over a long ridge 7,500 ft above sea level. During this part of the walk, we were joined by two Samburu tribesmen. We strode along at their pace. They covered the ground with an easy, graceful stride which seemed unhurried, but ate up the miles at an incredible rate. I had seen a milepost where they joined us, and had also noted the time. The tribesmen left the road after an hour, by which time we had passed seven mileposts. After the tribesmen had disappeared up a footpath, we sat down and rested for twenty minutes to recover.

After our rest, we marched down a smooth red earth road that meandered through a lush forest. Black-and-white Colobus monkeys made warning calls as we intruded on their domain. Brightly colored birds flashed across the road, and through the overhanging trees we could see birds of prey wheeling about an azure sky. We arrived at Meru at about 11:30pm on a Saturday night, very tired and unable to do anything but find a place to collapse. We heard the sound of a party, and found a crowd of revelers at the Pig and Whistle Hotel. There was nobody from whom we could scrounge beds for the night. The hotel was supported on wooden pillars, and we crawled under the floor to sleep all night, through the noise of the party. Waking chilly and starving, we opened the second and last can of corned beef, before setting out for Isiolo, the furthest point of our trek from Nairobi.

We arrived late in the evening, and were offered a hearty meal by the District Commissioner (D.C.). He also found accommodation for us in the Chief of Police's house. The policeman was away so we had the house to ourselves. We rose very early, and took advantage of a warm bath, changed our clothes, and washed out our dirty set. These we wrung out as best we could before attending breakfast with our friend, the D.C. Isiolo is situated in a very dry, flat area, relieved by a tree lined river that runs down from Mount Kenya. We saw camels employed to transport the local population on their migrations as they follow the sun in its travels north and south. The camels were loaded with all the accouterments of nomadic desert life including tents with their poles. These were partially erected like sails to give shade for the camel riders. The result was a very good representation of 'ships of the desert'. As the caravan silently passed us with the camels' noses in the air, spurts of dust were kicked up by the wide, rounded, partly cloven, padded, feet as they swung by with their peculiar gait with both legs on each side moving forwards and backwards in unison.

We faced a fifty-eight mile walk to Nanyuki, the first part of which was all uphill on a rough, stony road. We left Isiolo, shortly before 5am when the temperature was 52 degrees F, according to Bob's thermometer. We climbed steadily, and by 7:30am the temperature had risen to 96 degrees F. This temperature rise was very enervating and, by the time we reached the main Nanyuki road after a climb of 1,500 ft, we were very weary. But our laundry, which we had hung on the outside of our backpacks, had dried. We packed it, and trekked on like automatons. We were lucky to get a lift with a farmer for the last fourteen miles into Nanyuki.

No arrangements had been made for accommodation in Nanyuki, and we were lucky to meet an elderly lady, Mrs. Anderson, out for a stroll at about 8:30pm. She was very kind, and took us to the Silverbeck Hotel where she was a permanent guest. She gave instructions, and the cook prepared a wonderful mixed grill which we downed voraciously while talking to our hostess. She was not impressed with our forty-four mile hike from Isiolo to Timau, and claimed that, as a young woman in England, she had frequently hiked forty miles in a day. My silent guess was that forty miles in the English climate was not quite as arduous as forty-four miles in the heat and at the altitude we had encountered.

There was nowhere for us to sleep, but we found a steel-bodied International pickup truck. We climbed into the back of this, and settled down for the night. The front seat of the vehicle was occupied by the hotel's night-watchman. The night was icy cold, and the steel body of the pickup was very uncomfortable, so we evicted the night watchman, who was not supposed to be sleeping anyway, and climbed into the cab. Bob, being more a gentleman than I, lay across the floor of the cab, while I curled up on the seat.

All went well until about 2 am when the vehicle lurched forward several yards. Bob was lying on the floor-mounted starter-button, and the pickup was in gear. Bob quickly realized why we were heading out of the garage, and rolled off the button. We selected reverse gear, and pressed the starter button again to reverse neatly back into the garage. It was lucky that the garage was a drive-through shed, and we had not crashed into a wall.

After the disturbed night, we rose very early, still weary. Our hiking was now becoming tiresome, and we were concerned that we were becoming weakened and had doubts as to our ability to keep going without two or three days rest.

This was out of the question as we had little money, no food, and nowhere to stay. Our parents were expecting us back home in a day or so.

We decided that we should return to Nairobi without delay, and we hoped to find a lift. There was a tour bus parked in the hotel grounds belonging to the tour company owned by Tiny Gibbs. The tour bus was to return empty to Nairobi, so we asked the driver for a lift. He insisted that either we pay the full tourist rates or we phone his boss, Bwana Tiny. The phone was in a locked office and, while we tried to find who had the key, the driver took off without us.

We girded our loins and walked to Karatina. There was nowhere to stay in the small African village, so we decided to take a ride in a 'Banana Express'. These were buses, used by the Africans, and fares were cheap. They were always heavily loaded with up to twice as many passengers as they were legally permitted to carry. Bananas, bicycles, baskets of live chickens, sacks of vegetables and fruit were piled high on top of these buses, which raced from one stop to another, trying to beat any competing bus to pick up waiting passengers.

Blue exhaust fumes poured into the passenger compartment, and this had the effect of anesthetizing the passengers, who became sufficiently dopey as to ignore the perils of the otherwise terrifying journey. Together with the exhaust fumes was dust, which seemed to be sucked into the bus in great clouds. We both cat-napped as the bus hurtled down the earthen roads, tore round corners, and braked to shuddering stops to allow passengers to dismount and others to climb aboard.

Bob and I were regarded by our fellow travelers with friendly amusement. Europeans did not normally travel in Banana Expresses. We roared into Thika, and came to a brake-squealing stop. There was a police barrier across the road. Some passengers dismounted, and an African police-man peered into the bus and casually sauntered away. A

European policeman then appeared, and threatening us with a big revolver, barked at us to get out of the bus.

He was clearly determined that we should follow his order with alacrity.

Bob and I gathered up our dusty backpacks and climbed stiffly and wearily off the bus to face a very ferocious copper.

"Who are you?" he demanded.

Bob and I were still dopey from lassitude caused by an overdose of exhaust fumes, and may have appeared somewhat languid, and possibly, a little arrogant. We didn't say, "Who wants to know?" although it may have seemed that was our attitude.

"I'm Bob Winter," drawled Bob. "And I'm Len Gill," said I.

"That means nothing to me," shouted the irate copper. "Prove it. Who are you?"

"I'm Bob Winter," drawled Bob. "And I'm Len Gill," I rejoined.

"I KNOW THAT," screamed our inquisitor.

"Well, that's all right then." We turned to climb back into the bus, having apparently satisfied the Law as to our identities.

But this was not the case. The policeman hadn't even started, and was hugely annoyed by our apparent nonchalance. He waved his very big revolver in our faces, and asked his favorite question once again.

"Who ARE you? Prove it. Show me something that proves who you claim to be!"

Bob and I dived into our pockets, and were nearly shot for our troubles.

"*Keep your hands where I can see them,*" screamed our inquisitor. Bob and I took our hands out of our pockets, and stood, hands on hips, gazing at the suspicious cop questioningly.

"Just how are we supposed to present proof of our identities if you object to our searching our pockets for docu-

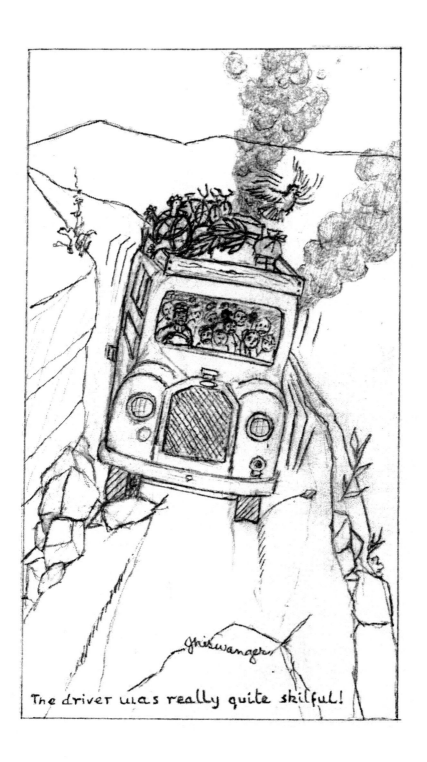

The driver was really quite skilful!

mentary evidence?" Bob asked. "If you deny us permission to search, how do you expect us to verify our claims?"

Bob's manner of speech seemed to convince the policeman that we were not villains. He allowed us to reach into our pockets again. Bob showed him a crumpled telegram from his father, but all I could come up with was a well-thumbed, creased photo of Joe, my little dog.

The cop wanted to know where we went to school, and our fathers' occupations. Bob's Dad was a bank director, and my Dad was the head of a well known lumber business. On learning this, the policeman became rather more docile, and began to show subservience by calling us 'young sirs' and bowing.

"Very dangerous to travel by Banana Express, young sirs," he commented, bowing.

"Oh, they are not as bad as they might seem." I remarked, "The drivers are actually pretty skillful."

"Don't you know about the escapees? Haven't you heard the news, young sirs? Six Jews have escaped from Gilgil. I really thought I'd captured two of them." He chuckled and bowed. "You will understand my disappointment, young sirs." Smiling self-depreciatingly, he bowed again.

The copper was being friendly. It was my turn to be suspicious. Our bus had driven off without us, and there seemed to be something in the policeman that indicated amusement at our expense. He explained that there were Jews trying to get from various European countries to Palestine, but the Brits were firmly opposed to this idea. So, the Royal Navy was stopping all ships headed for 'The Promised Land', and the poor wretched refugees were being incarcerated in concentration camps, one of which was at Gilgil in Kenya. There had been a dispute, and the camp commandant had become adamant in his refusal to concede to the internees' demand. Consequently, they had threatened that six of them would escape, unless their demand was granted. Since it wasn't, six Jews duly escaped. They were never recaptured. Bob and I, having provided sufficient proof that we were not Jews from Europe, were free to continue our travels.

Our now-fawning policeman explained that we had been seen walking through Karatina, and he had rushed to set up a road block when it was reported that we had climbed aboard a Banana Express heading for Nairobi. He was sure we must be strangers in Kenya as Europeans don't travel in 'Banana Express' buses. He now gave orders for the road block to be dismantled, and walked off toward his big, shiny police car.

"How about a lift into Nairobi?" Bob and I called after him. "Our bus has gone, and we have no money left".

"Sorry, young sirs," the despicable cop yelled over his shoulder. "No can do. Civilians are not allowed to ride in police cars." He was grinning broadly, satisfied that he had finally shown who really held the power.

"BASTARD!" Bob and I screamed, as the police car accelerated away down the thirty-five mile road to Nairobi.

We plodded on. We were now in poor condition, and no amount of loin-girding enabled us to do anything but trudge pitifully the last thirty miles homeward. Literally staggering the last three miles, resting for a few minutes every quarter of a mile, we arrived at my home at about 10:30pm. My parents were out, and we raided the larder. With every muscle aching, we polished off a loaf of white bread cut into thick slices, smeared with butter, and liberally smothered with Lyall's Golden Syrup. This was followed by cups of tea as we sprawled in the lounge.

As soon as we had finished our snack, Bob leapt to his feet, and said he must start for home. I couldn't believe him. Twenty minutes earlier we had been so tired that I had wondered if we were ever going to reach my home. Now Bob was determined to cycle some eight miles to his home. Brooking no argument, he mounted his bicycle and peddled away.

I wandered back into the house and washed the dishes. I didn't hurry since I was waiting for my parents to return. I thought I'd better phone Bob's parents to tell them their son was cycling home, and that he was very tired. It might be some time before he reached them. I was amazed to learn that he had already arrived, and had crawled into bed after taking a shower. He had taken forty minutes to do the eight mile trip the last mile of which was up a steep hill.

My parents arrived home, and I gasped a greeting before inching my way upstairs and falling into bed. I slept for twelve hours, and even then could only mumble the tale of our adventures to my parents. We had covered a total of some 400 hundred miles in nine days, the last day of which we had walked over seventy miles, and had traveled in the Banana Express about 50 miles. We had each spent the equivalent of about $1.50, being the cost of our ride in the bus. The energy we had spent was recouped within a day or so, such is the bounce of youth.

Reflecting on our trek, I realise that we were not real travelers. We had barely noticed our surroundings. We had ignored the possibility of game watching. We were disinterested in the people whose farms and villages we passed through. Birds were for the birds, and we were deaf and blind to them. The beauty of the country went unobserved. We were conscious only of the heat of the sun on our shoulders, the ground under our feet, the strain of climbing hills, and the grinding trudge needed for daily progress.

What did we get out of the ordeal? A great sense of achievement. We had learned our limits. We were satisfied with this.

12

Again the Sap Rises

Sometime later, in my sixteenth year, I met the lovely Ann Stevensen. Typically Scandinavian, she was a blue eyed blonde with a figure that had every male between the ages of ten and one hundred panting. I escorted her to private parties, collecting her from her parents' house, and returning her there on or before the appointed hour set by her mother, a crusty woman. Her mission in life seemed to be to prevent her daughter from enjoying herself. I suppose she thought that she was protecting Ann's virginity but, if that was her mission, she didn't know her daughter, who was a naturally modest girl.

I ran foul of Mrs. Stevensen when I took Ann home after a party, and failed to see her close the front door behind her. Well, there didn't seem any point in hanging around. I hadn't even been rewarded with a goodnight kiss, Ann being disinclined to encourage anything approaching salacious conduct. Mrs. Stevensen insisted that seeing Ann to the door and leaving her there was simply not good enough. In future I was to escort Ann to the door, and wait until she had gone inside and closed the door behind her. This is what a young gentleman was supposed to do - not just drop her off and skedaddle like a mannerless moron.

Mrs. Stevensen had a way with words - which embarrassed her daughter, but was like water off a duck's back as far as I was concerned. What really cooled my ardor was an entirely different matter. Ann's mother accused me of deliberately choosing the site of the men's restrooms for our new sports club - directly opposite her lounge window, 150 feet away on the other side of a main arterial road.

A group of ex-Prince of Wales School boys had decided we should have a sports club. An ex-army office building, 50 ft by 30 ft, was being auctioned, and the club organizers bid for it. Their bid was accepted, and they then learned that the wood building had to be removed within a few days. Volunteers were recruited with the promise that those who put in a certain amount of time would be acknowledged as founding members of the Old Cambrians Club, as it was to be known. As founding members, they would not have to pay entrance fees.

Taking the building apart proved to be a bigger problem than had been expected. However, we managed and the dismantled parts were transported to the Club's site for re-assembly. The organizing committee had purchased an ideal area for the club off a main road opposite to the Stevensen's bungalow. Slowly the building took shape in spite of many difficulties arising out of the employment of volunteers who had no building skills. The committee members became impatient and testy.

The building had been an office, and certain amenities had not been included. There were no privies. A sports club for men and women would certainly need privies. We volunteer builders could have done with a privy when we were busy creating problems. But the committee decided that a Committee Room was of greater urgency. One end of the building was walled off and equipped with furniture. Non-committee members were banned from this sanctum, which became a refuge for surly organizers to hide from disgruntled workers seeking immediate answers to ever-rising problems.

Happily, the organizing committee was able to raise money from supporters of The Old Cambrians Club. They could now see that a club house was well on the way to completion. Funds with which to buy materials and sanitary ware for privies became available. It was decided that the privies be built some yards from the main club house - directly opposite Mrs Stevensen's lounge window.

I was a little surprised at the siting of the restrooms, wondering what folk were supposed to do if they had to go out when it was raining heavily. But the privy building was completed and put into service.

"I cannot think what induced you to build the lavatories directly opposite my lounge window," complained Mrs Stevensen when I went to collect Ann one evening.

"I had no say in where the building was to be sited," I was getting a little tired of Mrs Stevensen's constant complaining. She ignored me.

"I would have thought you would have had greater consideration."

"But..."

"Look at him. It is just too obvious what he is going to do," snapped Mrs Stevensen.

I looked out and saw a slightly inebriated Old Cambrian making his way hurriedly to the privy undoing his fly in readiness. Mrs Stevensen had a point. I took the matter up with the organizing committee, and was rewarded with the construction of a covered walk from the club house to the restrooms, which satisfactorily screened traffic to and from the offending building. But I was also excluded from free entry to the club. It was evident that I was friendly with members of a vast anti-club conspiracy. I'm not sure who dropped whom, but my platonic relationship with Ann ended abruptly.

13

Trinity College, Dublin is about to be graced

I left school in 1948 at the age of seventeen to attend Trinity College Dublin, Eire. I viewed my entry into Trinity College with trepidation. I was to attempt to qualify as a Bachelor of Science in Chemistry, Physics and Mathematics. My education in these subjects was deficient, and, though I had passed my end-of-school exams, they were indifferent passes. But Dad was adamant that I should follow in his footsteps. I felt he was wrong, but was unable to change his mind. Both Dad and Mum were excited about their only son's entry into university, and spurned my own reservations as to my competence.

Dad took me over to Dublin, saw me installed in digs, and the start of my university life. I had a great deal to learn over and above my studies. I had to find my way around Dublin and the university. Dad bought me a sports bicycle with down-swept racing handlebars, odometer, and lock. Dad and I explored Dublin and the surrounding area by taking bus rides to the end of the routes, enjoying a meal in a local eatery before returning to downtown Dublin. After ten days, Dad departed for Kenya, leaving me to learn how to react to those I met, how to manage my finances, how to organize my laundry, where to make purchases, where to eat meals, since breakfast was the only meal included in the rent charged for my digs .

I found that I was far behind my fellow students in all the subjects we were studying and, in an effort to make up lost ground, I sat up night after night poring over my books with a sense of panic. This worsened when I found that I could read and understand, but couldn't even remember what subject I'd been studying as soon as I put the book away. My eyes started to give trouble, and I went to have them checked. They were perfect but tired very quickly - within seconds of starting to read. I was advised to cut down on studying, which I felt I could ill afford to do. Everything seemed to be piling up. My studying was ineffective, and I was getting further and further behind.

The lecturers were not of much help. My main trouble was in advanced mathematics. We had two lecturers, and both were deemed geniuses in their subject. The problem was that they simply couldn't understand why anyone couldn't grasp the pure logic and beauty of mathematics. I found the subject tortuous and impractical. One lecturer was extremely sarcastic, while the other lived in a world of his own, and raced through explanations making no attempt to check that we were following him. The fact was that neither of them could teach, and were too impatient with those of us who were wallowing in a mire of confusion.

One of the two lecturers had come to Trinity College as a boy of fourteen. He had been admitted on the strength of his genius at mathematics. I went to see him in his rooms where he had lived for nearly half a century. The university had been built during the time of Elizabeth I of England, who reigned from 1558 to 1603. I doubt that the professor's rooms had been cleaned or redecorated from the time the building was completed, so, by 1949, they had a distinctly 'lived in' look - except that the professor hardly lived. It was more of an existence than a life. An old, cheap, wooden table stood in the center of the room, groaning under the weight of stacks of yellowing papers, the lower layers of which hadn't been looked at for many years. One heavily stained corner of the table was clear of paper, and on it stood a dirty, cracked mug containing an inch of cold tea.

The walls of the building were very thick, and on a window sill stood a filthy gas ring, under which there was a thick mat of rancid fat which ran down the wall. The professor's unmade bed was covered with gray sheets and a noxious blanket. The rooms had a fetid odor, and one could imagine lice, fleas, rats and mice being happy co-residents, undisturbed by the mathematics professor. I felt it unlikely that the professor would be able to understand the problems of a dense student.

The professor cycled each day 150 yards from his rooms to the lecture room on a rusty old machine that had never seen a drop of oil. I used to watch him as he rode round corners, lost in a maze of calculations which described the segment of the parabolic curve he was negotiating, and the centers of curvature thereof. He was unable to enlighten me in any way about the problems I was facing, and I was loath to spend more time in his foul room.

Our chemistry professor took interest only in completing each lecture with a minimum of interruption. On one occasion a visiting university rugby team was to play our boys on a field close to the chemistry lecture theater. The game was to commence at 5 p.m. and we all hoped that the professor would rush his lecture a little so that we could race to see the match. Five minutes before the lecture was due to end, precisely at 5 p.m. a number of students began closing books and snapping pencil-boxes shut. After a pause, he said with heavy sarcasm, "Ladies and gentlemen, I still have a few pearls to cast." He finished his lecture at 5 p.m. precisely. Trinity College won the match.

***

One of my student friends was also having trouble with his studies, and suggested that we take a complete break during the summer vacation. He went off to enjoy his pastime of photography while I went cycling, rambling, bird watching and swimming. I also spent a week with another fellow student at the popular resort of Dun Laoghaire on the coast some seven miles south of Dublin, where we took a basement flat. I spent most of the time swimming at one of the several men-only bathing points. Ireland was still a bit prudish in those days, and mixed bathing was still a new concept. My pal entangled himself with the remarkably attractive daughter of a hardware store proprietor. He saw more of her, in more than one sense of the word, than he did of the basement flat. But he was always on hand at breakfast time to make us Welsh Rarebit, at which he was expert. He maintained that a good sized Welsh Rarebit, followed by a few more slices of toast and marmalade and a mug of tea to wash it down was all that he needed to last him through the day, but I suspected his diet included the fruits of love.

As the summer came to an end, I felt guilty at having taken time off from my books. I cycled back to my digs, and returned to my studies with renewed determination and desperation. I was a little fitter, and my eyes were better. But the break solved nothing in the long term, and I was faced again with the panic I had been experiencing before the interruption. I felt sick at heart, and contemplated ending my life. It would be easy to swerve suddenly head-on into the path of a bus speeding at 60 mph along the coast highway. I was diverted from such a course by thoughts of the anguish that my family would suffer. I decided to plow on to the best of my ability, hoping that my constant study would, in the end, bear fruit. I hoped in vain.

The Bull of Limerick

During another vacation, I spent two weeks with a student pal in Limerick. Frank had inherited a pub, called

The Bull, with an apartment over it. This he had furnished with furniture bought at an auction, when the contents of a local mansion were sold. He had an exquisite grand piano in walnut, and a matching oval dining table with eight chairs. These were included in one lot, together with several mounted African gazelle heads and Zebra and Colobus Monkey skin floor mats. The lot had cost him less than the equivalent of $20, which compared with the amount I spent in two weeks to enjoy a student's life.

Frank was the second son in the family. He had volunteered to serve in the Royal Air Force during WWII as the tail gunner of a bomber, and had caught a burst from the machine guns of a German fighter. He was badly wounded in his thighs but made a miraculous recovery. During the war, his parents had died and his older brother, who had also volunteered to serve with the British forces, had been killed.

So Frank returned home to take over the pub, which was a very popular one, and earned himself the nickname 'The Bull' after his pub's name. He also earned himself the right to go to university, all expenses paid by British taxpayers. He employed an honest young man to run the pub, which provided a net income for The Bull of about $600 a month - a handsome amount in Eire in those days.

The Bull took a three year course in history, and passed the first two years' examinations with ease. Thereafter he deliberately failed the finals so that he could continue to enjoy the largesse of the British. I was told by a fellow student of The Bull's that he was able to correct the lecturers if they erred, but so enjoyed university life that he ensured that he failed his final examinations. After I left TCD, I heard that the university eventually insisted that The Bull either pass his finals or quit. So, he passed the tests, and earned himself a good degree.

When I stayed with The Bull in Limerick, we did a good deal of hiking. On one day we covered forty miles, and returned to the pub to down a considerable amount of non-alcoholic cider. Neither of us indulged in alcoholic drinks.

The following day, in need of a rest, we went to a hospital to visit a friend of The Bull's, another pub owner.

The Tiger of Limerick

We found Tiger O'Brien sitting up in bed. He was about 60 years of age and looked good for another 60 years. What ailed him, I never discovered. Tiger was heavily muscled, having been a member of the Limerick Rowing Eight in 1908, and a keen rugby player. He had biceps of twenty-one inches circumference and his chest was so deep that the sheets and blankets couldn't be tucked in under the mattress over his body. When we went into his private ward, he had just returned from a stroll. The doctor had advised him not to go too far, so Tiger had limited the length of his walk to fourteen miles.

Tiger left the hospital a day or two later, and over the next few days we met him at a local restaurant. This was a large room with a mezzanine gallery above the ground floor. The roof was in the form of a curved glass arch, which let in the summer sun to light up the ground floor. It was the custom for men to take seats under the gallery and await the arrival of the office girls, who came in daily at about 10am. They enjoyed sitting in the sun-lit area, where they came under the scrutiny of the boys lounging around on the 'side-lines'. I had never believed that the girls in one area were more beautiful than those in another, but the Limerick girls were gorgeous. Dubliners tended to be short. At just a tad under 6 ft 2 inches, I was nearly always the tallest person in a Dublin crowd. The girls in Limerick were tall, beautiful and elegant. I didn't really notice the men.

One evening, Tiger asked me to accompany him to a rugby match. He was on the committee of a local club, and the match was an important one, though not well attended. The evening being very chilly, everyone wore overcoats. We stood on earthen terraces with a few other spectators. Two or three terraces below us were two men discussing a matter which had split the rugby club's committee. They were both big men, obviously rugby players. I heard one man say "Yeah! And Tiger O'Brien, he's another of the bastards."

Now Tiger was not one of the most mentally alert, so several seconds went by before he stepped down the terraces, and tapped the fellow on the shoulder. He turned, and a look of horror spread over his face. Tiger grasped the lapels of the petrified man's overcoat in one fist and hoisted him up, so that his feet were dangling off the ground.

Tiger then shook the man saying "Don't forget the tiger came out of the jungle!" before depositing the terrified man back on terra firma. Tiger took his place beside me again. It was said that, if a customer became belligerent, Tiger would walk quietly from behind the bar, grasp the offender by his collar with one hand and his belt with the other and literally carry him to the door from where he cast him sprawling into the street.

Frank, the Bull was also a big man, but he never seemed to have trouble from his customers. This was possibly because The Bull allowed poker to be played in the back room of the pub, and since gambling was illegal, nobody wanted to attract the attention of the Garda, as the police are known. So they behaved themselves. The stakes were low, and there was considerable whispered argument which became more intense as the Guinness flowed. I suspect that the Garda were happy to allow quiet gambling to take place, as it kept some of the ruffians off the streets.

Upstairs, in The Bull's apartment, more serious poker was played by a select few who were invited. Here the stakes were much higher and the chatter much less - the money doing the talking. Frank, being in receipt of a good income, could afford to play aggressively, and I saw him on several nights pick up $400 to $800. He also played poker at university, where the sons of the wealthy regularly enabled Frank to more than double the income from his pub. I found card games and gambling extremely boring and didn't participate. But I enjoyed watching his rivals squirm on their seats as The Bull won hand after hand.

Frank enjoyed motorcycling, and had a much desired Triumph Speed-Twin, on which he rode to Limerick on weekends to relieve the manager. He had two motorcycling friends, who were twins.

One Easter Frank invited these friends down to Limerick to stay at the pub. Returning to Dublin on the evening of Easter Monday, they rode in single file, with Frank bringing up the rear. At exactly 6pm, as they approached a bend in the road, the leading twin hit a patch of ice, skidded across the road, and impaled himself on the iron railings of a churchyard. He died in agony.

Exactly a year later, to the minute, Frank and the remaining twin were returning to Dublin, when his pal hit an ice patch at the same place and killed himself in exactly the same way as his twin brother. Frank sold his motorcycle.

Dropping out?

After the break in Limerick, my eyes were better for a while, but I was still unable to retain what I studied. The old panic returned, and I tried to ignore the fact that I couldn't remember what I'd been studying a moment after putting the book away. I pressed on in the hope that, somehow, I had absorbed something. But my marks for the end-of-year examinations were dismal.

The fact of the matter was that I was studying the wrong subjects. Probably I was not university material, and would have been better at a polytechnic in a hands-on mechanical engineering course. The authorities at TCD apparently agreed that I was wasting their time, my time and Dad's money, and I was 'sent down' - a euphemism for 'kicked out'.

I 'folded my tent', packed my bags, sold my books, and winter clothes. I set out for a shop where they sold used bicycles. A gale was blowing sleet across the road and I cycled as fast as I could pedal with my head down. I smashed into the rear of a van breaking bones in my right hand, right collar bone and my sternum. Fortunately my bicycle was not damaged and I was lucky to get a good price for it as the shopkeeper must have been suspicious. My face was ashen and couldn't help but make occasional whimpering sounds from the pain that wracked me.

Having no time to bother with medical attention, I booked a flight to Kenya by way of London and suffered agony whenever I had to handle my baggage or face customs officials. During the flight I sat huddled in my seat in mental, emotional and physical anguish. I despondently faced a painful meeting with Dad and Mum. I had let them down ignominiously. I had wasted Dad's money. I had nothing to show for months of hard study. Would they believe that I had tried? Or would they think I'd idled my time away and squandered the funds Dad had provided for my education. Could I ever re-pay his generosity? Would I ever be able to redeem myself in my parents' eyes?

When she saw me, Mum realised that I was having problems lifting my cases and Dad insisted he carry them out to the car. Mum asked me what was wrong and took me to see a doctor as soon as she could arrange an appointment. My injuries diluted the disappointment she and Dad must have been feeling. When she saw the badly broken collar bone as I took off my shirt to be X-rayed, Mum was horrified. No X-ray was necessary. There was little the Doctor could do. He thought everything would heal after the bones had realigned themselves. He was right but for the bones in my hand which were to break again several times. Eventually bits of bone had to be removed.

14

Dad's parents

Grandpa Leonard was born in 1860 and Grandma Maud in 1869. At the age of twenty-one, Dad had left home in 1912 for Africa because he couldn't get along with his parents. His father was a genius, and lived in a world apart from the rest of the human race. Grandma was indubitably the most unpleasant person I ever met. She had been born in Canada, and Dad thought her mother died in childbirth.

Maud's father, a ship owner/skipper, was also of an unpleasant disposition, and was unpopular with his crew. So much so, that one day when he was climbing up a cliff on a rope ladder, someone stamped on his fingers when he reached the top. His last word was "Ouch!" as he put his squashed fingers in his mouth. To do this he let go the rope ladder and gravity sealed his fate. He fell back sixty feet onto the deck of his ship, which made an awful mess of his fo'c'sle. It didn't do him much good either. It's possible he fired off an expletive – "Oh shit!" a split second before he hit the deck, but the story is silent on this point.

Grandma and her sister, Fan, were now orphans, and were shipped off to England, where they were raised in a convent. Why they were sent to England, we don't know, but I suspect that the Canadians had had enough of the family.

Like many geniuses, Grandpa Leonard was unable to comprehend that others had difficulty understanding some of the things that seemed so obvious to him. But he seemed to take a liking to me, and told me something of his early life. His father had been a surgeon in the days when the profession was only beginning to emerge from an occupation performed by quacks. Surgeons also served as barbers. It is an interesting point that he once severed a leg at the thigh in thirty-two seconds - which is the time it took our Company Sergeant Major to shear my hair when he decided that I would never make a soldier unless my hair was restyled to a shaven, bleeding bare scalp.

From the age of nine, Grandpa Leonard assisted his father. In those days gin was cheap, and was used to get the patient drunk before the operation was performed. Anesthetics were known but gin was cheaper, and possibly more fun for the surgeon if the patient passed out before he finished his ration of gin. But the whole business was rather a messy affair with the patient vomiting and bleeding all over the place. No doubt it was Grandpa's job to clean up after each operation.

By the time Grandpa turned fourteen - in 1874 - he'd had enough, and he gave up medical practice to join a firm of civil engineers. They too were considered charlatans. Until they started in business about 1830, all civil engineering projects were designed and supervised by architects. Civil engineers now began to specialize in the design of bridges, roads, docks and similar structures. The firm that Grandpa joined was one of the first, and had been established for some 44 years. He was to make a significant contribution in the field of civil engineering, and designed bridges for China and for the Indian and South African railways. His modular design for docks was still used many years after he retired in 1914 following a row with the British Admiralty. He developed civil engineering formulae after proving that the formulae the architects had been using were incorrect.

Consequently designs called for excess materials and tolerances.

He took an interest in poetry, and could recite from memory, many classics - and quite a few salacious rhymes too. Another of Grandpa Leonard's interests was shorthand writing. He learned five different types and developed his own. When he died at the age of ninety-two in 1952, he was believed to be the oldest fluent speaker of the artificial language, Esperanto, which was expected to become the world's lingua franca.

When we discussed his early life, I asked Grandpa if he regretted anything that the modern world was improving. The only thing he could think of was that the quality of newfangled pencils had dropped. Modern pencils were, in his opinion, rubbish. The softness or hardness of the lead did not conform to the designation marks on the pencils. His eyesight was not what it had been, and pencils of the softest designation failed to make marks that he could see.

Dad conferred with the doctor who was attending Grandpa and Grandma. The doctor's opinion was that neither of them would survive another winter in England. So Dad, without conferring with Mum, flew them out to Kenya in 1949 when Grandpa was 89 and Grandma was 80. Both were frail, though Grandma Maud was still able to be as unpleasant as anyone that ever lived, without actually causing grievous bodily harm. Grandpa Leonard died in 1952 at the age of 92, but Grandma Maud lived on until 1963 when, at the age of 94, she finally gave up making Mum's and my sister, Margaret's, lives a misery.

Grandma Maud was one of those who consider it clever to be critical, and typical of the type, did very little beyond the minimum to keep alive. This ensures that they do not attract criticism of themselves. She could condemn succinctly. Sunday lunch was usually a roast, and if it was chicken, which was not her preference, she would peer distastefully at it as she entered the dining room and pronounce, "Foul."

On one occasion Mum took her up on this critical remark by saying "You don't have to have any if you don't want it."

Grandma retorted, "Who said I don't like it?"

"Well the way you looked at it, and the way you said foul, made me think you'd rather not have any," said Mum.

"I said fowl meaning a bird, not foul meaning unpleasant," claimed Grandma, but we all knew exactly what she had meant by the look on her face. She then dug in, and consumed everything Dad put on her plate. It was just that she preferred roast beef, pork or lamb. But Mum could not always afford these more costly cuts.

The house my parents had when my Grandparents arrived from England was in Muthaiga, the snobby area of Nairobi. The house was two storied, and the staircase had no landing, but curved sharply back on itself. The stair treads tapered to nothing on the inside of the curve. This was obviously too dangerous for my aged Grandparents. So Dad bought another house.

Mum never liked the new house, mainly because it was not in Muthaiga where her parvenu would-be friends resided. The new house was rambling, single storied and ideal for the old folk. The main bedroom was 27 feet by 18 feet. Their beds were at one end, and a couple of lounge chairs and a coffee table were placed at the other end. There were plenty of built-in cupboards and a good sized en suite bathroom. A wide bay window looked out over the three-acre grounds.

Mum and Dad entertained often. The idea was that the old folk could retire to their room for their evening meal when there were guests, and would not have their routine interrupted. Grandpa couldn't contribute to any social gathering as he was rather deaf, and neither he nor Grandma understood much of the conversation, not knowing the subject or people under discussion. They were both rather untidy eaters. Grandpa was inclined to dribble and Grandma tended to drop food onto the table, down her chest and onto her lap. But she always insisted they join the party.

She would glare at the clock on the mantelpiece as her supper time approached. While the guests enjoyed a sundowner, Grandma constantly asked what time dinner was to be served. Mum replied sharply, "When it is ready," or "When we are ready to eat." Grandma had, all her life, enjoyed her evening meal, high tea, at about 6 p.m., but in Kenya, this was too early as the evening could be too warm to enjoy a meal. So, we normally sat down to dinner at 8pm when the day was cooler.

To avoid Mum's sharp response, Grandma would lever herself up from her chair, totter over to the clock, peer closely at it and then at her watch. If it was past her usual supper time, she would heave a deep sigh, and totter back to her chair. She would then keep glancing at her watch. Her behavior perplexed the guests, and Mum had to refrain from tearing her hair out at Grandma's heavy prompting.

My sister, Margaret, was in her teens when Grandpa and Grandma arrived in Nairobi, and such was their attitude toward young people that Margaret felt she could never ask her friends to the house. Her life was severely disrupted by our Grandparents, and she entered her twenties as an exceptionally naive and immature girl.

I was lucky in that I had become a selfish, inconsiderate boor, and chose to be as unpleasant to Grandma Maud as she was to me. I was quite capable of using foul language when arguing with Grandma Maud when we were alone, and this shut her up faster and tighter than a clam, to Mum's unenlightened approval. She never realized why Grandma was keeping her trap shut, and behaving like a disgruntled bull dog, while I was happily wandering about whistling tunelessly. I was gratified that Mum was happy.

I was fond of Grandpa, and was sorry that I hadn't met him before he became senile. Since his retirement in 1914, he had developed an endearing, puckish sense of humor. For years he had endeavored to learn something every day. Some subjects he studied for months while others, like poetry for instance, for but a few minutes. His brain had remained active well into his dotage, but had begun to wane after his stroke in 1948. His relationship with Grandma appeared to be one of master to servant. He barely noticed her presence, but she obeyed his every whim. I gained the impression that he had been extremely assertive in his younger days.

15

Good-bye TCD. Hello, again Kenya

My time at university was not entirely wasted. I returned to Kenya in 1950 at the age of nineteen, a humbled young man, now more than ready and eager to get down to a job.

Dad had now more or less washed his hands of me. He suggested that I go to see the headmaster of my old school, the PoW. 'Pink Percy' Fletcher had taken up the job of headmaster of the PoW after the end of WWII, and had proved to be a dynamic, no-nonsense, professional with a record of having sorted out pretty tough schools in England and New Zealand. His nick-name came from his florid coloring, resulting from his healthy lifestyle.

I doubt that there was anybody on the planet more suitable for the job he had to do. As students, we respected him from the moment that he set foot in his office, and we came to admire him as he boldly sorted out problems, abolished unnecessary rules and restrictions that were difficult to enforce, and were frequently ignored. Pink Percy inspired self-discipline leading to self-control. He had always regarded me with a jaundiced eye, and rightly suspected that I was one of the more idle and aimless members of society. But I was sure that he would give me good advice to put me on an appropriate path.

I approached him with some apprehension. I was going to have to admit to my abysmal failure at university which would bear out all his opinions of me. I had made an appointment to see him, and he was awaiting my arrival. He came out to greet me, ushered me into his office, and invited me to sit down. He sat opposite me and opened with, "Hum! Gill. Hopeless at mathematics. What can I do for you?"

I explained my position and my painful failure at T.C.D. He must have sensed that I was truly humbled. He seemed to feel that the school had failed me, and that he personally should be held responsible. We argued this point for a few moments. He had come to the school only shortly before I left. It was hardly fair to hold him responsible for the years during which I had developed into a feckless lout. We agreed to disagree on this point, and turned to the question as to what path I should now follow.

He opined that I enter commerce, and should seek employment with a large enterprise which offered proper training. I applied to an oil company and an import/export firm, and was accepted by the latter. Dalgety & Co. Ltd. was an Australian firm with an office in the City of London which supervised the East African branches. I'm sure that Pink Percy had a lot to do with the company accepting me, and I'm sure there was no better organization in which to start my commercial life.

***

Dalgetys had a scheme that offered trainees experience in a number of different departments. The firm was chiefly concerned with the export of agricultural produce, but offered farmers and planters an exceptionally wide range of services and equipment in order to attract their export business. Farmers and planters joined co-operatives managed by the company. The co-ops offered financing, accounting and insurance services and agricultural produce marketing expertise. Over the years some sections of Dalgetys, which were not strictly allied to the agricultural industry, had been developed. Examples of these were an office equipment department, a wines and spirits department, and a travel department.

The General Trading Department offered to obtain anything that a farmer or planter might require for his estate. I was posted to this department to learn the difference between a cash sale slip, an invoice, a credit note, a journal entry slip and a pro-forma invoice. We negotiated trade discounts on everything we bought. The discounts were shared equally with the farmer. If the company negotiated a 40% discount off the retail price of an item a farmer required, the farmer paid 80% of the normal price. This meant that the department didn't need to hold stocks of a huge range of items but could offer virtually anything a farmer or planter needed at a discounted price, and retain a small mark up. The farmer's account was settled when his crop was sold by Dalgetys. In the General Trading Department I bought and sold everything from a bottle of aspirin to an International TD 24 crawler tractor, at that time the largest of its kind on the world market.

***

One day a planter's wife came in and asked me to get her a dozen towels. After I had gained experience, I would have asked for a detailed specification of the towels she wanted: color, type and size. But with an air of confidence, I noted 'Towels' on my list and, as soon as my customer left, I scooted round to the department store from where I had stolen a small toy cannon years before. I entered a section of the store that seemed appropriate and approached a rather cheerless young lady shop-assistant.

"A dozen towels, please." My businesslike terseness matched her demeanor, I thought.

"Bath sheets, bath towels, guest towels, hand towels - or sanitary towels?" she barked. The last type seemed to me to be that of a fairly general type of towel.

"Sanitary towels, I suppose. I mean.....I think......er.....she didn't say what........." I stammered.

"I suggest that you find out then. Sanitary towels will be useless if your customer wants bath towels. Do you know what sanitary towels are?" There appeared a glint of merriment in her eyes, which increased my embarrassment. Had I known what sanitary towels were, I would have died.

"I'd better find out," I mumbled, turning to flee.

"Yes, I think you'd best do that." I sped out of the store followed by peals of laughter.

Eddy's Episodes Expand my Training

Eddy was an irrepressibly ebullient salesman in the Office Equipment Department. He was, perhaps, inclined to be a touch irresponsible, and took great delight in teasing his female colleagues. They felt safe from unwanted advances from Eddy who was apparently more attracted to men. The Travel Department was managed by a very efficient, older woman, whose staff were all very decorative young ladies of good background. Being decorative was of greater impor-tance that being brainy, or so it seemed, and the young lovelies were an obvious target for Eddy's teasing.

Occasionally a customer would leave a passport with the Travel Department, and one in particular was sent round to most departments in the building, as it contained the most un-passport-like photo ever stuck in a British passport. It is well known throughout the world that a passport photo is supposed to make the holder look like a criminal. Not just a nefarious character, but a scoundrel of the worst type.

The holder of this passport was one Lady Celestine Fairfield-Ffoulks. Her photo showed her wearing a tiara, looking coyly over a mink-stole-covered shoulder. A triple string of pearls was visible, and the hand that held the stole was adorned with three very ornate jeweled rings. Passports in those days gave somewhat more detail of the holder than they do today, and the name of the holder was on the first page inside the front cover. There was a line entitled 'Occupation' but this was not always filled in. After all, some women might be happy with the title of 'Housewife', but Lady Celestine would certainly not be happy with such a mundane description. So, the space was left blank.

Eddy decided that it should be completed. He gazed at the photo for a long time, and then opened a bottle of permanent black ink. He practiced copying the penmanship of the British civil servant who had carefully entered the details which Lady Celestine had deigned to allow to be entered in her passport. When Eddy was sure that he could make the entry in the very same style as the rest of the entries, he carefully completed Lady Celestine's passport.

Much mirth was heard around Dalgetys as the passport was passed around. I didn't approve of Eddy's alteration, but supposed that Lady Celestine would be unlikely to notice the description. After all, who actually looks at their own passport? And most immigration officials around the world usually merely glance at a passport, raise their eyebrows, and hand the passport back without comment.

But supposing Lady Celestine fell foul of the law in some foreign country. Lady Celestine appeared to be a person who liked to party. Suppose she had a glass or two of Champagne too many, and in a fit of exuberance knocked a French policeman's kepi off. An excess of 'Bubbly' can make some folk prone to that sort of innocent, light-hearted prank. You can never tell how a policeman will react to a frolicsome female who knocks his hat off. What is he going to say when he demands the lady's passport, and learns that she is a - Prostitute?

***

131

I was transferred to the Office Equipment Department where there was a shortage of staff due to Eddy being away on 'home leave' in England. I managed to secure two very substantial orders, but found myself unpopular with Eddy when he returned from leave as sales revenue had increased substantially during his absence. Eddy thought himself to be an outstanding salesman because of his popularity with customers. I knew that he could be bitchy to those who overshot his sale figures, so I decided it might be politic to participate in one of his more harmless practical jokes.

We closed at noon on Saturdays. One Saturday, when the Travel Department staff were anticipating a happy and joyous weekend with their latest gentlemen friends, Eddy phoned through to the department and, in a thick German accent, introduced himself as Doctor Vogelsheitz (Birdsh*t) wanting to book a passage on a ship, due to leave Mombasa imminently, for New Zealand.

Dr. Vogelsheitz insisted that he wanted to travel to Mombasa by train. He had heard about the overnight passenger train trip to Mombasa, and travel by train was one of his great loves. He also wanted a certain cabin on the ship, and was adamant that Dalgetys make these arrangements immediately, as the ship was to leave the following evening. Dalgety's travel department was to phone the German Ambassador in Nairobi when all the arrangements had been completed. The German Ambassador would personally pass the message on to Dr Vogelsheitz.

On Eddy's instruction, I had already phoned through to Dalgety's Mombasa Travel Department, who had to work that weekend due to a flurry of arrivals and departures. I told them what was required and they gleefully agreed to play their part.

The young lovelies in the Nairobi Travel Dept. got to work. They phoned through to Mombasa branch, and were told by their colleagues that they would try to book the passage. It was pointed out that Nairobi was very late in trying to make the booking; it was very hot in Mombasa, and it was a Saturday. The Mombasa staff seemed a little indifferent to Nairobi Travel Dept. demands. Nairobi Travel Dept. personnel went ballistic. This booking was important. Dr. Vogelsheitz was a friend of the German Ambassador. He may even be his boss. Mombasa had better get moving.

Meanwhile, another decorative young lady in the Nairobi Travel Dept. was trying to arrange, by phone, Dr. Vogelsheitz's overnight train trip to Mombasa. This was proving difficult. The Asian railway booking clerk asked if it was possible for the young lady to come down to the station. Then everything could be sorted out as soon as payment was effected.

"But we don't want to pay yet. We….."

"Sorry, Madam. No payment, no ticket." The clerk knew his job.

"No. No. You don't understand. We…."

"But Madam, I do understand. You no pay, no ticket. It is against the law to travel on the train without paying."

"Yes, I know that." The young lady was getting a bit hot under the collar - or whatever decorative young ladies get hot under. "I have to check first whether we can get our customer on a ship going to New Zealand."

"Sorry Madam. We do not operate ships. For this you must deal with a travel agent. We deal only with travel by rail. But you have to pay."

Mombasa hadn't phoned back. Nairobi thought it time to chase up those dopey Mombasa staff. No they still had no news about the passage to New Zealand yet.

Y - a - w - n. "I'll have another try. But you do realise that you've left it a bit late and today, after all, is Saturday. I'm supposed to be playing tennis this afternoon."

And so it went. Hour after hour. Dalgety's Nairobi Travel Department staff was having a very bad day. Finally, at about 5:30pm all was arranged. They phoned the German Ambassador.

"You vont to speak viss whom?"

"Well, I'm not sure that I'm pronouncing the name correctly but I want to speak to your friend Dr. Vogelsheitz."

"Do you sink you are being fonny? I know of no one mit such a stupid name. Now get off my phone, immediately." The phone was slammed down in a very undiplomatic manner.

At this moment Eddy, with me slinking a few feet behind him, walked into the Nairobi Travel Dept, giggling fit to burst. A hail of pencils, pens, stapling machines, phone directories, handbags and high heeled shoes were hurled at Eddy's head.

The Tale of the Typewriter Mechanic

After six months, I had learned all about card index systems, filing systems, stock record systems, adding machines and calculators, accounting and dictating machines and typewriters. I also learned that the senior mechanic in the Typewriter Repair Section, Mr McGreedy, was paid a basic wage plus a commission on monthly turnover. He claimed repair times which, if added up, showed he worked at least twenty-five hours per day, every day of the month. He earned a higher income that anybody else in the Company, much to the chagrin of Mr. Kent, Dalgetys C.E.O. But there was little to be done. Mr. McGreedy had signed contracts written by the company. We received no complaints from customers, and the Typewriter Repair Section was extremely profitable.

Mr. McGreedy's considerable earnings led to envy and unpopularity amongst the rest of Dalgety's staff. He was also rudely curt and arrogant in his dealings with both customers and colleagues alike. He used to gamble on the British football pools, and he could well afford to spread his bets. Consequently, he frequently won small amounts, and took care to let all and sundry know of his skill in completing the weekly football coupons using complex mathematical permutations. He refrained from telling us how much he spent in comparison to his winnings.

One event that Mr. McGreedy did not brag about was told in a tale we managed to piece together with help from Effie, Mr. Kent's secretary, and her sister, Marvie, secretary to the boss of The Bumper Pools Agency, with whom Mr McGreedy placed his business. Both had overheard most of the conversations since their offices were adjacent to those of their bosses' and had communicating windows. Mr McGreedy's assistant typewriter mechanics filled in parts of the narrative, and a little conjecture glues the pieces together.

One day at about 9:00am Mr McGreedy received a phone call from the manager of the football pool agency in Nairobi.

"Is that Mr McGreedy?" asked the caller.

"Yes, this is Mr McGreedy. Who is calling and what do you want?" snapped McGreedy.

"Mr Max McGreedy?"

"Yes! This is Mr Max McGreedy. What do you want? I'm a busy man. My time is valuable. Just get on with it."

"Well," said the caller, "this is Kingsley Campbell-Hunter, Manager of the Bumper Football Pools Agency."

"And what can I do for you Mr Kingdom Campdown-Blunder? Or whatever your name is."

"I'm very pleased to be able to inform you, Mr McGreedy, that I have just received a cable from the U.K. to say that you have won second dividend on last week's football pool."

"How much?" barked McGreedy.

"I'm afraid I can't divulge that information over the phone."

"For God's sake, why not? I've told you who I am. This is Mr McGreedy, Mr Max McGreedy. Tell me how much I've won."

"I'm afraid I can't divulge that information over the phone."

"Second divi, you said. It must be a large amount. Gimme some idea."

"Yes. It certainly is a substantial sum."

"How much?"

"I'm afraid I can't..........."

"Yes. Yes. So you said before. But surely you can give me some idea."

"I have told you, Mr McGreedy, it is a substantial sum. I am now leaving my office, and will be with you as soon as I can." Mr. Kingsley Campbell-Hunter rang off abruptly.

Mr. McGreedy sighed with impatience, and tried to get on with his job, but his mind wasn't on it. He waited for an hour, and then rang the football pool agency to find out "What the hell is going on?" A young lady told him sweetly that Mr. Campbell-Hunter was on his way.

Another hour went by and McGreedy called the agency again. This time he was told, just as sweetly, that Mr Campbell-Hunter was on his way, but had to call in at the bank to obtain a certified check, as the amount of McGreedy's win was so large. No, she couldn't divulge the amount over the phone.

McGreedy slammed down the phone and strode upstairs, and burst into the office of Dalgety's C.E.O., Mr. Kent.

"You can stuff your bloody job!" he yelled at a startled Mr. Kent.

"I beg your pardon, Mr. McGreedy."

"I said, you - can - stuff - your - bloody - job!" Bawled McGreedy again.

"Mmm. I thought that's what you said. What's brought this on?" inquired Mr. Kent politely.

"I've just been told by Mr. Campbell-Hunter I've won second divi on the football pools. So you can stuff your bloody job." McGreedy was smug. Though he earned the highest salary of all Dalgety's staff in East Africa, he still felt the need to tell the boss of the Company what he could do with his job.

"How much?" asked Mr. Kent.

"They are not allowed to divulge that information over the phone," said McGreedy tiredly.

"Not even about how much?"

"A substantial amount, they told me."

"How much is a substantial amount?"

"They're not allowed to divulge that information over the phone."

"Second divi, you say?.....It could be a very large amount.......On the other hand.......What do you think a substantial amount might be?.....Second divi could run into hundreds of thousands.....He wouldn't be allowed to say......" Mr. Kent was speaking more to himself than to McGreedy.

"I was told that they were not allowed to divulge...."

"Yes. Yes. So you said before." Mr. Kent seemed to be following an earlier conversation. McGreedy experienced an eerie sense of flashback.

"I think I'd advise caution," said Mr. Kent. "This is what you should do McGreedy." McGreedy hated it when people omitted the 'Mr'. It made him feel like an oppressed worker. Mr. Kent continued. "Go downstairs to your workshop and get on with your job until Mr. Campbell-Hunter lets you know just how much you have won." McGreedy, still incensed by Mr. Kent's omission of 'Mr' responded assertively.

"So, you advise prudence? Well, you can still stuff....."

Something made him stop. Something his mother used to say: 'Always err on the side of caution.'

"....if the amount is substantial," he ended lamely.

"Yes. Well. Off you go, McGreedy. Let me know how things stand after you've spoken to Mr. Campbell-Hunter." He shooed McGreedy away by flapping the backs of his hands at him. McGreedy took half a pace forwards and seemed about to say something, but his mother's advice was ringing in his ears, he turned and strode out of Mr. Kent's office, slamming the door behind him.

"Uncivilized bastard," muttered Mr. Kent to himself.

Mr. Kingsley Campbell-Hunter had been vexed by McGreedy's utterances earlier that day, and had deliberately delayed his arrival at McGreedy's workshop with the bank certified check for the largest amount that any of the agency's customers had ever won, in a sealed envelope. He arrived just as McGreedy was about to leave for lunch. He proffered the envelope to have it snatched from his grasp. With trembling hands, McGreedy ripped open the envelope and stared at the check. He tottered backwards, caught himself, turned a sickly ashen color and gasped.

"A substantial amount? I earn more than this in a month! A substantial amount? Good god! This is a paltry amount."

"I understand you to be a typewriter mechanic, Mr. McGreedy. I thought you would think the amount substantial."

McGreedy began to turn from wan to purple. He brushed past Mr Campbell-Hunter, stormed up to Mr. Kent's office, peremptorily knocked, burst in, and threw the 'substantial' check on the desk. Mr. Kent picked it up, smiled and said, "I did advise caution. Go back to your work and we'll say no more about the matter."

McGreedy hesitated. He seemed to expect Mr. Kent to offer condolences for the sorry amount, but Mr. Kent was having problems. He flapped his hands at McGreedy again and, as he quietly shut the door behind him, that unhappy man heard Mr. Kent burst into peals of laughter. As he turned from the door, he heard Mr. Kent chuckle, "Five hundred and twelve pounds. What a caution!"

Mr Campbell-Hunter was surprised to learn of the level of pay earned by Dalgety's typewriter mechanics, and sent his company's typewriters elsewhere for servicing. McGreedy was humble - for several days.

Glass: I face The Grim Reaper again

The salary Dalgetys paid me while I was under training was very low, so at the age of nineteen, I was still living with my parents.   Elizabeth had finished her nurses' training, had married, and was living in South Africa. Margaret was in England training to be a children's nurse. Mum and Dad decided to visit Elizabeth. It was to be the adventure of a lifetime, as they were to drive down from Nairobi to Pietermaritzburg in Natal, a distance of about 2,000 miles, over some of the worst roads in Africa. They planned to be away for four months.

I moved into an inexpensive hotel, sharing a room with an elderly gentleman, Mr. Webster, who had just lost his son. A bulldozer blade had fallen on him when a hydraulic hose burst. The son, a few years older than I, had been at school with me, and his sister had been at school with Elizabeth. So, we had known the family slightly for some years. Mr. Webster, mortified by the tragic death of his son, was lost in a world of grief. We spoke to each other very little, only politely greeting each other as occasion demanded.

One morning I went to breakfast on the verandah overlooking the car park at the front of the hotel. I was feeling mildly off color. I helped myself to some fresh fruit, and sat at a table on my own. I took a mouthful of fruit and swallowed. I suddenly felt very ill. The fruit was immediately ejected with considerable force. Sweat broke out on my brow, and I felt shaky. The symptoms were unusual, and I thought that perhaps the mother of all migraine attacks was beginning. I returned to my room and lay on my bed.

I remember nothing of the following few weeks. I can only suppose that Mr. Webster helped me to the toilet, and must have got water down my throat. I had no idea how long I had been ill when I was shaken awake to find three men standing over me. One was my god-father, another was my boss, and the third turned out to be a doctor. They had been in conversation with Mr. Webster, but he had not been very helpful as he was still distracted by the death of his son.

The doctor asked me a few questions, but I wasn't helpful either. But I did remember being violently sick after taking a mouthful of food. How long ago was that? I had no idea. Nor did Mr. Webster remember how long I'd been sick. The doctor gave me a tablet and a glass of water. I washed down the tablet, but it too was ejected with extreme violence. I was very embarrassed, but the doctor gently told me not to worry, cleaned up the mess and said he would be back. I think he came back the following day, but it may have been later the same day. I had no idea of time.

He gave me a tablet to chew, and surprisingly I was not sick. He left me with a box of tablets, and told me to chew one three times a day - morning, noon and night. Together, he and my god-father visited me daily, and my recovery was miraculous. Within three days I was eating. I suffered no pain, and kept all my food down. My weight had dropped by over seventy pounds. Now I began to put on weight at the rate of about a pound a day. Soon I was well enough to go to the doctor's surgery in town where I underwent test after test. I had barium meals and x-rays. I had to take samples of my urine and stools. My blood was checked. All seemed OK. So I had all the tests over again. In vain the doctor tried to find the cause of my illness. I returned to work and learned that I'd been away for nearly three months. I had to report to the doctor weekly for more tests. One day he told me that he had not been able to come to any conclusion. He had thought that I'd had a burst duodenal ulcer, but the tests didn't confirm this diagnosis. He told me that there was no need for me to see him again, unless something went wrong. If anything out of the ordinary occurred, I was to contact him again, day or night. I left his surgery.

As I walked along the street, I had a flashback of memory. I raced back to the surgery, and burst into the doctor's room. A naked lady skipped behind a screen.

"Well. What is it?" asked the doctor sitting in a chair at his desk.

"I've just remembered. I swallowed some glass accidentally."

"You bloody fool! Why didn't you tell me?"

"I'd forgotten about it....I'd forgotten all about it." I was dazed and amazed that the incident had gone completely out of my mind.

"Now I understand." The doctor was thinking as he spoke. "What happened was that the glass lacerated your duodenum. You may not have noticed when you passed the glass. Possibly, some time later, the lacerations became septic and you became very ill. Like a person with a burst ulcer suffering from peritonitis. But it didn't show up in the x-rays as the duodenum was generally lacerated. There was no localized injury, as in the case of an ulcer. Now I understand."

He rose from his chair and put his hand on my shoulder. "I think we've got to the bottom of your problem. Off you go. Don't swallow glass again. You've been very ill. You're lucky to be alive.

"I'm sorry I burst in like that. But it came to me in a flash, and I just had to tell you."

"I'm glad you did. Don't worry about it," said the doctor kindly.

"Don't worry about it," said a voice from behind the screen.

I walked back to my office remembering the incident. Shortly before my parents' departure for South Africa, I had taken four friends in Dad's car to see a film. It proved to be extremely boring, but having paid, we saw the film through to the bitter end. We smoked all the way through, and were dying of thirst when the film finished at about 11:20pm. We walked to a hotel where coffee was served until midnight. My pals had ordered coffee but I wanted water. The coffee came but not the water. I again ordered a glass of water, but again it didn't come. And again and again, but no water.

At mid-night some of the lights were turned off, and I caught the eye of another waiter, and explained that I had ordered water several times to no avail. I told him that the hotel manager would soon come round, and when he asked what we were doing sitting in the gloom, I'd tell him that the waiters had refused to bring me a glass of water. The waiter sped off and returned with a glass of water.

I grabbed it and gulped it down. Huh! The waiter had put ice in it. I had swallowed some of the little pieces. Good I thought, and took another gulp. A large piece stuck in my mouth. Funny, I thought. It's not cold. I drew the piece out and to my horror found it to be a segment from the rim of a broken tumbler.

I conjectured that someone had knocked over a tumbler on a table and it had broken. A waiter had probably brushed the broken pieces off the table into another tumbler, and carried it to the sink. The waiter who eventually served me had filled the tumbler with water from a faucet without washing out the glass, and brought it to me.

I had read that very day in the Readers Digest that anyone who swallowed glass would die within fifteen minutes. I explained things to my pals, took the keys of Dad's car from my pocket, and instructed them that when I died they were to put my corpse in the trunk of the car, run me home, waken my parents, and explain what had happened.

Then we waited. Nothing happened, other than my pals becoming white with worry. I ran my pals back to their homes, and went back home to bed. The following day I was still alive. So much for the medical article in the Readers Digest, I thought. What with my parent's imminent departure for South Africa, and my going to live in the hotel, I never thought about swallowing glass again until after being so ill. Perhaps the article in the Readers Digest had said glass swallowers died after about fifteen days, not fifteen minutes.

For years I suffered from the after effects of the injuries, but I never got around to suing the hotel for millions, as we didn't do such things in Kenya.

Hellish Pains

From about the age of eight, I had suffered from terrible migraine attacks which blinded me and gave me unbearable headaches that nearly led to a loss of consciousness, caused difficulty in enunciating some words and numbness in my fingertips. Each attack lasted for two or three days, during which I repeatedly told Mum I wished to die. I was to suffer from these attacks for years. Then in my late teens, I learned that many people are allergic to cheese, that had often been served with macaroni at school; chocolate, a treat that we had during school vacations; coffee and red wine. I too was allergic to these foods. If I was prudent in their consumption, I avoided the attacks, which then occurred only at times of extreme worry, stress and emotional upset.

When I was about twenty-one, a pharmacist, who also worked for Dalgetys, but in a different department, gave me a sample of a Burroughs Wellcome product which completely changed the nature of the attacks. I no longer suffered the stunning headaches, and my vision was not as badly disturbed. Each tablet contained a massive dose of an ergot compound with an added antihistamine to counteract the nausea that the ergot would have otherwise induced. Perhaps those Burroughs Wellcome tablets so controlled the attacks that my system 'forgot' how to do them. Whatever happened, I have been forever grateful to the pharmacist and to Burroughs Welcome. The reduced intensity of the attacks and their shortened duration has made them far more bearable.

***

I was moved to another department. This time I was to spend time in a warehouse where stocks of hardware, fertilizers, insecticides and fungicides were stored. I helped in the prompt execution of dispatch instructions and the quick off-loading of railway trucks to avoid demurrage charges. It was hard, often dirty work, and I'd end work-days reeking of blood-and-bone-meal fertilizer, or covered in cuts and scratches from handling fifty-six pound coils of barbed wire or twenty-eight pound bales of sharp *pangas* (machetes).

Another job arose when a general strike was called. I got to be a strike breaker when I drove an International van on butter deliveries. All our African employees were off work. Most had reported for duty, but there was a lot of violence against those who worked, so Dalgetys took the names of all those who reported for work each day, and then sent them away. After the strike was settled, they were paid. Those who had failed to report were not paid on the assumption that they had supported the strike.

I was instructed to help with deliveries of butter to shops around the city. I had to load the van with wooden cases, each containing fifty-six one-pound packets of butter, drive around town from one customer's store to another under instructions from an Indian storeman, and off-load cases in accordance with the customer's requirements. The van was unmarked, and the load could not be seen, so we were not approached by strikebreakers as I drove about the city. Trouble threatened when I off-loaded consignments in the street, before carrying them into a customer's premises. Being taller and stronger than average, and with a bit of humorous badinage, I turned aside attempts of intimidation. The strike ended after a week, but it heralded more serious discontent.

The Mau-Mau Emergency Looms

After a few months in the warehouse, I was posted back to the General Trading Department where I had first started my commercial management training. I had been there for a few weeks when the Mau-Mau rebellion loomed. From 1946, political agitation had excited unrest, principally among an element within the Kikuyu tribe, the largest in Kenya. In 1949 the name Mau-Mau first appeared, and by 1951 the movement had taken hold in the Kikuyu tribal areas.

Murder and mutilation of Kikuyu families were added to the menu of inducement to join the movement. In an attempt to force otherwise peaceful Kikuyu tribesmen to take the oaths, senior Kikuyu personalities who opposed Mau-Mau were kidnapped, tortured, mutilated and assassinated. European families on isolated farms were also subjected to these atrocities, and their cattle were maimed or slaughtered, and farmhouses, buildings, and crops were burned to the ground. Terrorist threats of death and the administration of obscene oathing ceremonies persuaded even the most reluctant to join the proscribed Mau-Mau society.

In 1952 reports were circulating in government offices, raising alarm at the breakdown of law and order in many areas of Central Kenya. But not many settlers were fully aware of the situation since the Governor of Kenya, in an effort to end his tour on a good note, tried to keep the lid on reports of growing unrest.

At the time, my life was in turmoil. I had fallen for a delectable, pulchritudinous, blonde who sent my desires into a whirling welter of lust. I was distracted from everything but my out-of-control passions and craving to cavort with abandon. But gradually I became aware of the world beyond my enchantment, and what I heard filled me with repugnance and anger.

Murders by Mau-Mau terrorists of progressive Europeans who encouraged African education, medical welfare, political advancement and greater participation in government by Africans, began to awaken the settler community to the jeopardy threatening the Colony. The Mau-Mau could not tolerate opposition by people of the Kikuyu tribe or progressive European benefactors.

A successful raid was executed by a gang of Mau-Mau on the Naivasha Police Station, when arms and ammunition fell into the hands of the terrorists. This was followed by a Mau-Mau massacre and ghastly mutilation of over one hundred Kikuyu women and children at the village of Lari.

These events blew the lid off the seething cauldron. I, like the majority of the population, was sickened and enraged by the atrocities. The newly appointed governor declared an emergency. Settlers were drafted into the Kenya Police Reserve. An on-going army training scheme for the sons of settlers provided a corps of full-time militia. They were to fight the terrorists, train a loyal Kikuyu Home Guard, and take up government administrative duties in the Mau-Mau terrorist dominated areas.

It was as though the stench of putrefaction rose from a morass to pervade the emotions and attitudes of usually rational people. Its progress fractured the fragile mutual respect that had been burgeoning among the diverse communities. The hideous hatred of *fatinas* (feuds) among Kikuyu people, Africa's chronic tribalism, and rancorous racism reappeared in full force.

A fight against terrorism erupted. My life was to change as I became involved in the battle. My lustful liaison languished, overtaken by the more urgent desire to avoid being killed...............

My next book, "Military Musings", takes us through the Mau-Mau Rebellion, a difficult and dangerous time for both the white settlers and the majority of the Kikuyu and other tribes who wanted no part of terrorist activities.

In the midst of war, I experienced moments of humor and the gentle sensitivity in the relationships formed both by accident and intent.

I hope you, the reader of this book, and my first book, "Rambunctious Reflections", will contact me with your comments and questions. I can be reached by e-mail at banner@rof.net or by mail at PO Box 2141, Glenwood Springs CO 81602, USA

- Leonard J. Gill

GLOSSARY

Swahili. (Properly Kiswahili). The *lingua franca* of East Africa. The language developed over several hundred years when Arab slavers dominated the area. There is no Swahili tribe. A *Mswahili* is a *Kiswahili* speaking person. *Waswahili* are *Kiswahili* speaking people. The language has origins in the languages of the coastal tribes of East Africa and Zanzibar, Arabic, Persian and Turkish. It has also borrowed from English, Hindi, German and there are traces of Portuguese. Arab slavers from Oman, Egypt, Saudi Arabia, Persia, Jordan and Syria operated, in safety, from the islands of Zanzibar and Pemba off the coast of Tanzania.

Kiswahili has five vowels each of which has only one sound:

A as in c<u>a</u>r; *E* as in g<u>e</u>t; *I* as ee in kn<u>ee</u>; *O* as in f<u>o</u>r; *U* as oo in b<u>oo</u>k. Diphthongs of two vowels are pronounced by running the two vowel sounds together as in the following examples: *Nairobi; shauri; tao,; toa;*

Ch as in chicken. *Th* as in thick. *Dh* as th in there.

The penultimate syllable is always stressed. Kiswahili words employ suffixes and this alters the pronunciation:

M<u>e</u>sa - table. *Mes<u>a</u>ni* - on the table. *Ch<u>u</u>mba* - room. *Chumb<u>a</u>ni* - in the room.

Words borrowed from Arabic, English and other languages do not use suffixes:

Ndani ya motoka - in the motor car (NOT *motokani*)

To simplify I have omitted the prefixes *M* and *Wa* in front of the names of tribes: *Kikuyu* instead of *Mkikuyu* - a Kikuyu person or *Wakikuyu* - Kikuyu people.

About the Author

Born in Kenya, East Africa, of English parents in December 1930, Len lived there until 1989. During his childhood, among his family and African servants, he ignored the dismay he caused them.

He enjoyed life. Even a period at boarding school offered Len scope for devilment. His absence at school relieved those at home of the complications that always seemed to attend his presence. His school teachers and friends had to bear the burden.

By the development of youthful arrogance, and in blissful ignorance of the vexations he caused, he was unaware of the necessity to balance humor with seriousness.

Africans dubbed him with the nickname *Mpenda raha* (he who enjoys a good time). Len insists that a shot-glass of humor helps the worries go down.

The inspiration in his life, Kaye, recognised Len's flair for storytelling, and insisted that, having reached three score years and ten, he get down to writing his memoirs.

Len now lives in Glenwood Springs, Colorado with his wife, Kaye and Shih-tzu, Bandit.

ISBN 1553956655-9